The Visitor's Guide
to
ICELAND

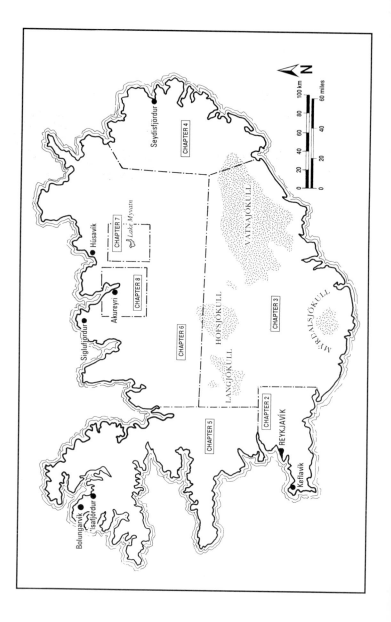

THE VISITOR'S GUIDE TO ICELAND

Don Philpott

MPC

Published by:
Moorland Publishing Co Ltd,
Moor Farm Road,
Airfield Estate,
Ashbourne,
Derbyshire DE6 1HD
England

British Library Cataloguing in Publication Data:
Philpott, Don
    The visitor's guide to Iceland. — 2nd ed.
    1. Iceland - Visitor's guide
    I. Title
    914.91'2045

ISBN 0 86190 299 8 (paperback)
ISBN 0 86190 298 X (hardback)

1st Edition   1985
2nd Edition (fully revised and redesigned)   1989

Colour and black & white origination by:
Scantrans, Singapore

Printed in the UK by:
Richard Clay Ltd, Bungay, Suffolk

Cover photograph: *Dettifoss* (MPC Picture Collection).

Illustrations have been supplied as follows:
MPC Picture Collection: pp 15, 19 (inset), 30, 31, 38-9, 70-71, 74 (both), 78 (both), 79, 82, 83, 90, 95, 106, 107, 115, 118 (bottom), 119, 126-7, 131, 134-5, 138-9, 142 (both), 146, 147, 150-51, 155, 166-7, 185 (both), 189, 198, 199, 202-3, 206, 214, 215; D. Philpott: pp54, 59; B. Pyatt: p75; H. Race: pp 14, 18-19, 22-3, 26-7, 34-5, 42, 110-11, 114, 118 (top), 210; G. Sveinsson of BSI Travel, Reykjavík: pp 58, 62, 86-7 (both), 91, 99, 111 (inset), 122 (both), 123, 159, 162-3, 170, 171, 174, 175, 194, 207.

The author and publisher wish to acknowledge the assistance given by YHA Adventure Shops and Icelandair in the preparation of this book.

CONTENTS

Key to Symbols Used in Text Margin

♣	Parkland	⌂	Church/ecclesiastical site
π	Archaeological site	⊞	Building of interest
🦌	Nature reserve/Animal interest	🏛	Museum/Art gallery
🦆	Birdlife	🏔	Beautiful view/scenery/Natural phenomenon
✴	Gardens/Plant life	⛷	Winter sports
⚑	Golfing facilities	✺	Other place of interest

Note on the maps

The maps drawn for each chapter, while comprehensive, are not designed to be used as route maps, but rather to locate the main towns, villages and places of interest.

FOREWORD

I celanders everywhere are fiercely proud of their homeland, and when they live abroad do their utmost to act as ambassadors for their country. So I am particularly pleased to have been asked to write the foreword to this new edition of the highly popular *Visitor's Guide to Iceland*.

Icelend is not cold and forbidding as the name might suggest, but a warm and friendly country, where the heat of the summer sun is only matched by the warmth of the people.

Iceland has so much to offer the traveller that it is surprising that not more people have discovered for themselves the charms of this lovely island - a land of constant contrast and change.

Don Philpott, although not an Icelander, has managed to capture the essence of this beautiful land of surprises, and his knowledge of the country portrayed in the book will be invaluable to any traveller.

If you fly in during the summer you can see the contrasts that make Iceland so exciting, the glaciers and the lava fields, the bustling fishing ports and fjords, the crystal clear rivers and lush green valleys.

Whatever the weather, there is no doubt that the climate is healthy and the country made for those people who want to get out and enjoy themselves.

While Reykjavík boasts many fine hotels, restaurants and shops, the real spirit of Iceland is best captured by getting out and discovering the constantly changing countryside. This guide helps you do exactly that.

Whether you want to walk or climb, birdwatch or swim, play golf or fish, pony trek or just laze, *The Visitor's Guide to Iceland* tells you where best to go and how to get there.

Iceland is a small country with a big heart and an enormous future. Once you have visited this fascinating land I am sure you will not be able to stay away.

Magnus Magnusson
1989

PREFACE

Iceland is a land of constant contrast and change. There are glaciers and ice-caps, volcanoes and hot springs, rushing streams and lush valleys. It is a large country with a small population and vast empty spaces that take your breath away with their beauty. It is home to spectacular waterfalls and the bubbling, spitting Geysir which gave its name to all the others.

As you fly into the international airport you can see why the Vikings called the country the Land of Ice. The largest glacier in Europe, Vatnajökull, dominates the island as you fly in. It is 8,400sq km (3,240sq miles) in extent and in some places the ice is more than 1,000m (3,280ft) thick. You fly in over the Vestmannaeyjar (Westman Islands) to the south, and steaming fissures which erupt periodically with uncontrolled ferocity can still be seen. In the north there are thermal springs and beautiful green valleys teeming with birds. During the summer there is permanent daylight and there is no pollution to filter the rays of the sun.

Iceland has still to be discovered as a tourist island although each year the number of visitors grows. Many tourists come here to walk over snow capped mountains, pony trek across lava deserts, play golf or simply relax beside a hotel pool somewhere different. There is something to do for everyone: sailing, fishing, climbing, birdwatching or just relaxing. The people of the Land of Ice are some of the most friendly on earth and a warm welcome is assured.

1
AN INTRODUCTION
TO ICELAND

History

Iceland gets its name from the first Vikings who arrived there in the ninth century, although Irish monks had been living there as hermits for some years previously. Certainly by the late ninth century there were several hundred monks living on the southern coast in the area of Kirkjubaer, and they fell easy prey to the bands of pirates that frequently raided. The first Viking settler is reputed to have been Ingólfur Arnarson who came from Norway in AD874. He established his home by the lake which is now surrounded by the capital, Reykjavík.

Over the next 60 years, until AD930, the Viking colonisation continued, mostly along the coast. As the Norsemen extended their control, the Irish monks were forced to leave. Iceland was, therefore, the last European country to be settled. The period between 870 and 930 was a time of a great colonisation. By 930 the island's population was certainly 20,000 and could have been double this. The Viking fleet sailed from Norway and entered and attacked many countries, including Britain and Ireland. Other vessels braved the Atlantic and stormed the Labrador coast while others penetrated the Mediterranean.

It was also a time of great conflict in Norway and there were many wars between rival war chiefs. Those defeated were forced to leave, and many sailed for Iceland to found a new kingdom. Their route took them first to Britain and Ireland, and many of the ships landed in Iceland carrying Irish slaves who had been rounded up to labour on the new farmsteads. Many of the Irish later earned their freedom and moved to the islands off the south-west coast where they farmed and fished — the islands being named after these men from the west — the Westman Islands (Vestmannaeyjar).

At the beginning of the tenth century the country was ruled by a number of chieftains and in 920 Ulfljót, one of the wisest and most learned, was chosen to travel to Norway to study its laws and system of administration so that a similar code could be introduced for Iceland. In AD930 the various chieftains gathered and formed the Althing, the country's first parliament, in the magnificent natural setting of Thingvellir, in a valley about 50km (31 miles) north-east of the capital. The Althing, or General Assembly, was a form of Icelandic Commonwealth made up of thirty-eight independent chieftains. A constitutional law code and a judicial system was introduced, with a Supreme Court held annually at Thingvellir. This form of republican government lasted until 1262 when Iceland became subject to Norway, and later to Denmark. Because Iceland was colonised so late, and perhaps because of the influence of the learned Irish monks, and later the Viking scholars, almost all the history of the island has been recorded. This documentation is found in the *Book of Settlements* and in the *Book of the Icelanders*, which were written in the twelfth and thirteenth centuries.

Christianity was introduced to the island in AD1000 from Norway, and over the next two centuries the pagan gods were gradually replaced by the Roman Catholic religion. The first bishopric was established in 1056 in the south of Iceland at Skálholt, and a second at Hólar in the north 50 years later. At both sites monasteries and schools were established, and they became the country's main centres of learning. The establishment of the monasteries saw the start of the period during which many of the Sagas were written.

In the late tenth century, Icelanders discovered and colonised Greenland, led by Eirík the Red. He had fled to Iceland after being banished from Norway, and his constant feuding earned him a further 3 years' banishment from the island. It was while he was in exile that he discovered Greenland. When he was allowed to return to Iceland he recruited settlers and together they sailed for Greenland where two colonies were established and survived until the fifteenth century, when the weather deteriorated and it became much colder.

At the turn of the millennium Icelanders sailed the North Atlantic to discover North America under the leadership of Leif Eiriksson, one of the three famous nautical sons of Eirík the Red. Despite this incredible achievement in 999, some 500 years before Christopher Columbus 'discovered' the New World, their attempts to settle there failed.

Towards the middle of the thirteenth century the fortunes of Iceland began to sink fast. The weather had turned much colder, crops failed and the fishing grounds were being 'robbed' by foreigners. The Commonwealth-style government collapsed and civil war broke out. In 1262 Iceland came under Norwegian rule and a new monarchial code was introduced in 1271, the Agreement of Union which had been concluded between the Althing and the king. It was to start 500 years of oppression under foreign rule. Just over a century later, in 1380, all the Scandinavian countries swore allegiance to Denmark and the King of the Danes reigned supreme.

In 1349 the Black Death struck the country wiping out at least a third of the population. The Plague struck again in 1402 and for 2 years ravaged the country killing again, at least a third of the inhabitants, and wiping out entire communities. It was in the first part of the fifteenth century that English traders started to visit Iceland regularly. They wanted to buy dried fish which until then had not been exported to any large scale — the main income being derived from the export of cloth spun from the wool of the island's hardy sheep. The English traders bought huge quantities of cod and this sparked off a change in the island's economy, and a dependence on fishing that still exists today.

Traders from many parts of the world visited Iceland, but less welcome was a band of pirates from Algeria who, in 1627, overran the island of Heimaey, slaughtering most of the islanders and carrying off the rest as slaves.

Under Danish rule the people of Iceland were forced to convert to Lutheranism, and both bishoprics were occupied by foreigners in the fourteenth and early fifteenth centuries. Between 1540 and 1550 all Church property was confiscated and handed over to the king. The Danes also imposed their own trading regime on the island which drained money out of the country and into the coffers of Denmark; in 1602 the Royal Trade monopoly was established.

Absolute monarchy was imposed in 1662 and all governing power was transferred to Copenhagen. For the next century the fortunes of the island continued to decline because of the repressive trading methods and the progressive cooling of the climate. The eighteenth century brought smallpox, sheep diseases, two disastrous famines and the eruption of Lakagígar in 1783, volcanic activity from which lasted for 2 years. At least 9,000 people starved to death during the famines and thousands of farm animals were killed. By the end of the seventeenth century, the weather suddenly turned much harsher with winters so cold in 1695 and 1696 that even the sea froze. A census taken in 1703, the first ever undertaken, showed a population of about 50,000 of whom a fifth were beggars or dependants. By 1709 the population had been ravaged by smallpox and had fallen to 35,000. There was a brief recovery which was short-lived; there were famines in 1752-7 and 1783-5 and natural disasters, which caused poverty so acute that by 1787 the harsh trading rules were lifted and all subjects of the Danish king were given the right to trade in Iceland. The position was not helped by the blockade imposed by the English navy during the Napoleonic Wars.

In 1800 the Althing was dissolved but the independence movement in Europe was growing and in 1809 a Dane, Jörgen Jörgensen, backed by a London merchant, seized power in Iceland. His reign was short-lived, however, and he was quickly ousted following the arrival of a British warship. The struggle for freedom continued, and was led in Iceland by Jón Sigurdsson who lived from 1811 to 1879 and is now the country's national hero. In 1843 the Althing was allowed to meet again as an assembly and in 1854 all trade restrictions were lifted.

In 1874 the country celebrated the thousandth anniversary of the founding of the first settlement with a new constitution from the King of Denmark, King Christian IX, and the power to control its own finances. Effectively it brought about an end of the absolute rule and paved the way for home rule which was granted on 9 April 1904. The island's first co-operative had been launched in 1882 and the National Bank was founded in 1885.

At the end of World War I Iceland's sovereignty was accepted by Denmark, although it remained united with Denmark through the king. The millenary of the Althing was celebrated in 1930. The final ties with Denmark were severed during World War II. In May 1940 British troops occupied Iceland to protect North Atlantic sea lanes and prevent an invasion by Germany from Scandinavia. On 8 July 1941 the United States took over the defence of Iceland following agreement between the two governments. Later Iceland joined the United Nations as an independent state. On 25 February 1944 the Althing announced it was ending the Act of Union and this was supported by 97 per cent of the voters in the hastily convened plebiscite. On 17 June of that year, more than 20,000 gathered at Thingvellir to hear Jón Sigurdsson, the President of the Althing, declare Iceland a Republic.

The early 1970s were dogged by the 'Cod Wars' with Britain which resulted in Iceland declaring a 200-mile limit round her coast and excluding UK trawlers. The 200-mile zones have now been adopted by almost every maritime nation. Diplomatic relations with Britain were severed for a short time but the 'Cod Wars' ended in 1976. In 1974 the 1,100th anniversary of the first settlement was celebrated by the opening of the road over the widest glacial rivers south of the Vatnajökull glacier, thus completing the circular road around the island.

Geography and Climate

Iceland is situated in the North Atlantic Ocean almost equidistant from New York and Moscow. It lies between 63° 24' and 66° 33'N, and between longitude 13° 30' and 24° 32'W, and is the second-largest island in Europe after Britain. It is close to the Arctic Circle yet only one of its northerly islands actually lies inside it. The country has a total area of 103,000sq km (39,756sq miles) and a coastline of about 6,600km (3,700 miles). The island is 300km (190 miles) wide north to south, and 500km (300 miles) across from west to east, and there are scores of islands off the coast, although many of them are uninhabited. Four-fifths of the island is above 200m (658ft).

Geographically, Iceland is considered as part of Europe yet there is nowhere else on the continent with a similar climate. The north-east coast is affected by the bitterly cold waters coming down from the Arctic Ocean while the rest of the island is warmed by the Gulf Stream. Greenland is 285km (180 miles) away and closest to Iceland; Norway is 1,000km (625 miles) distant, and Scotland 798km (almost 500 miles). Iceland lies over a submarine ridge which joins Scotland and Greenland, and which prevents the cold water from the lower depths of the Norwegian Sea, which lies to the north and east of Iceland, penetrating southwards. The temperatures at the seabed

Lava and fissures resulting from volcanic activity are a common sight in Iceland

Geothermal activity

are much higher to the south and west than to the north and east of Iceland, as one branch of the Gulf Stream reaches up to the south coast and flows west and north around the island.

The Polar current reaches Iceland's north-east coast, resulting in considerably colder temperatures. The mean sea temperature in the coldest month is about 5-6°C (41-3°F) off the south and west coasts, but only 1-2°C (34-6°F) off the north and east coasts. The respective summer temperatures for these areas are 10-11°C (50-2°F) and 7-9°C (45-8°F) again being the lowest off the north-east coast.

With the exception of some narrow fjords containing large amounts of fresh water, ice is very rare in Iceland's navigational waters. However, the Polar current carries large quantities of ice and icebergs southwards along the east coast of Greenland. Wind and current can sometimes force this ice over into the Gulf Stream, which then carries it eastwards along the north coast of Iceland, where it can block the north and east coasts and produce Arctic conditions. During the present century, however, it has seldom been seen near Iceland.

Because Iceland is situated on the boundary between the temperate and the Arctic zones, winters are mild, but stormy and humid. The Reykjavík mean January temperature is about the same as in Copenhagen. Periods of severe frost are rare owing to the warming influence of the sea in winter. Summers are, however, quite cool although the temperature for the warmest months averages between 9˚C (48˚F) and 12˚C (53˚F). Warm days with temperatures of 20˚C (68˚F) or over are rare near the coast, though they occur more frequently in the sheltered valleys away from the wind where, however, night frosts occur more often. The highest temperature recorded in Iceland is just over 30˚C (86˚F) while the lowest recorded in Reykjavík in the last thirty years is below -15˚C (5˚F). Rainfall is high during all the seasons, with snow over the high grounds and in the north in winter. The southern slopes of the glaciers get most rainfall, while the least falls on the plateau north of Vatnajökull. The snow lies at a height of 1,000 to 1,500m (3,280-4,920ft) and above, being highest north of Vatnajökull. The valleys of the north receive only about half the rainfall of the southern areas.

Gales are frequent and change direction rapidly with the passing of the depressions coming from the west. However, the air is usually clear and pure and even distant mountains appear quite near.

The Icelandic climate is characterised by alternating calms and gales, thaws and snow, good and bad weather. As a general rule if it is fine in the south, the weather will be bad in the north, and vice versa. There is also an Icelandic saying which goes, 'If you don't like the weather just wait a minute'.

So it can be seen that Iceland is not, in fact, a particularly cold place. Of course, in the winter proper clothing is necessary to keep out the cold, but it is often possible to walk around the town even in late autumn with only a jacket for protection. If you travel north into the lush green valleys beneath Akureyri, the summer temperatures can be very warm.

Whatever the weather, there is no doubt that the climate is healthy. The winters are not as severe as in many parts of mainland Europe and it is not unusual for Reykjavík to have no snow throughout the winter.

In midsummer along the lowland plains the afternoon temperatures may get up to 15°C (59°F) which is just the right temperature for backpackers, walkers and campers. As the very clean air increases visibility, and the intensity of the sun's rays, it is very easy to get a beautiful tan after only a few days. In fact, the weather often feels much warmer than it actually is. The increased visibility can also be deceptive. It is possible on a good day to see the snow-capped tip of the glacier Snæfellsjökull from Reykjavík, even though it is almost 120km (75 miles) away.

A great advantage of being so far north is that during the summer, the sun is almost perpetually above the horizon so it never gets dark. The midnight sun is a sight worth seeing, especially in the north of the island.

The cool climate has another advantage in that it deters many of the insects and reptiles that can prove a nuisance in hotter climates. There are no snakes in Iceland, but for a couple of weeks in late July or August the midges can be a pest.

The special climate has helped to form the massive glaciers which occupy more than 11 per cent of the total area of Iceland. The essential requirement for glacier formation is that more snow should fall each year than can melt. Gradually the snow depth increases and it is compressed, and becomes ice. Vatnajökull is Iceland's (and Europe's) largest glacier covering 8,400sq km (3,240sq miles) and in places the ice is more than 1,000m (3,280ft) thick. By measuring the snow layer it has been found that on some of the glaciers in southern Iceland annual precipitation must amount to between 5,000 and 6,000mm (200 and 240in) or as much as 500mm (22in) a month. That compares with the monthly precipitation at Sandur on the north coast of only 30mm (1.2in).

Geology

One of the most exciting things about Iceland is that in geological terms it is a new country, literally being shaped as we walk around it. One day in 1984 in Reykjavík there was an earthquake which registered 3.7 on the Richter scale, while on the other side of the country Krafla erupted, as it had done every year for the previous 9

Sulphur, hot springs and mud pools at Námafjall

years. A 9km (5½ mile) fissure opened up and lava, smoke and dust was hurled hundreds of feet into the sky. Although the earth's crust is normally about 30km (18½ miles) thick, in Iceland it is only 10km (16 miles) deep and scored with deep cracks and fissures.

The enormous forces which still push and pull the island are caused by the movement of tectonic plates which meet beneath the country. These plates split and separated to form the continental land masses, and where they touch, areas of immense activity will usually be found. Iceland is one of most active volcanic countries in the world and there are about two hundred volcanoes, at least thirty of which have erupted since the country was first settled. On average an eruption still takes place every 5 years. Nearly every form of volcanic activity takes place somewhere in Iceland which is why it is so attractive to geologists. In 1783 the world's largest fissure eruption took place when Lakagígar erupted along its 32km (20 miles) of craters spilling lava over 565sq km (218sq miles). The gases and ashes from this eruption devastated farming, polluted the meadows and led to one of the greatest famines in the country with the loss of thousands of lives. The fumes and gases from this eruption are said to have killed three-quarters of all the sheep and horses on the island, and half the country's cattle.

Iceland is built up of volcanic material. The eastern and western parts of the country consist of tertiary basalt, comprising roughly half the total area, whereas the central parts consist of volcanic material from the Ice Age mixed with water, glacial and air deposits, the so-called Palagonite formation. Approximately 10 per cent of the total area is covered with post-glacial lava. There is now no volcanic activity in the basalt areas. The highest volcanoes are cone-shaped (Öraefajökull [2,118m or 6,950ft], Eyjafjalljökull [1,665m, or 5,464ft]), always having an ice cap on the top, while others are shield-shaped (Skjaldbreid) and rift-shaped volcanoes are common.

Some rifts are quite open while others are more or less closed, and when eruptions take place rows of lava and volcanic ash craters are formed. Laki, for instance, is a 25km (15½ mile) long row of 100 craters and the eruption in 1783 lasted for more than 6 months.

Hekla is an elongated mountain ridge superimposed on a short range of craters. It produces both lava and ash. The last major eruption, in March 1947, threw a column of debris and smoke 36,000m (100,000ft) into the air and the lava covered 64sq km (25sq miles). It is Iceland's most famous volcano and has erupted fifteen times. Throughout the Middle Ages it was feared throughout the Roman Catholic world as the Abode of the Damned. The 1947 eruption lasted for 13 months and in May 1970 a number of small craters on the mountain erupted throwing out lava for 2 months. The last eruption occurred in 1982.

Katla is a fissure covered by the Myrdalsjökull. The glacier melts during eruptions causing huge floods, explosions that rock the country and it rains ash that turns day into night. The production of lava is usually insignificant. Katla last erupted in 1918 but has erupted at least thirteen times since the first settlement of Iceland. It is said that when Katla erupts the flood water exceeds the volume of water carried by the Amazon river. Askja in the north-eastern highlands last erupted in 1961, but its eruption in 1875 was the last to cause great damage.

The most dramatic eruption of recent times occurred in 1973 and started in Heimaey, the only inhabited island of the Vestmannaeyjar (Westman Islands), on 23 January. The entire population of about 5,300 were evacuated to the mainland in a matter of hours without loss of life. The eruption lasted for almost 5 months and half the town was buried in the lava flow; the rest was covered in a thick layer of ashes. The island was the centre of the fishing industry, and the harbour and all its installations were saved by the quick action of scientists who poured cold sea water on to the lava which succeeded in halting the flow. Heimaey is one of the wonders of Iceland. The lava wall still hovers over the town and houses can be seen projecting underneath it. The greatest miracle was that the lava wall, more than 7m (20ft) high, came to a halt only feet from the hospital, and so it too was saved. Since the eruption most of the islanders have returned and it is once again a thriving fishing community.

Two types of lava are to be found in Iceland. *Apalhraun* corresponds to the Hawaiian *a-a-lava*, and has a rough, slaggy surface, while *helluhraun*, is similar to the *pahoe-hoe* lava, which is smooth and often has a rope-like surface.

Iceland consists mostly of mountains and high plateaux and its average height is 500m (1,525ft) above sea level. The highest point is Hvannadalshnjúkur in the Öraefajökull glacier in south-east Iceland at 2,119m (6,950ft). Post-glacial lava covers about 10,000sq km (3,861sq miles) and the largest lavafield is Ódádahraun, covering about 4,662sq km (1,800sq miles).

There are frequent submarine eruptions around Iceland and the

Glacial ice-caps cover approximately 11½ per cent of the country

most famous occurred on 14 November 1963 when three islands were thrust up from the ocean bed south of the Vestmannaeyjar. Two of the islands later collapsed, but the third remained and is called Surtsey. It has an area of almost 4sq km (1½ sq miles). The eruption continued for more than 2 years and the island is now closely guarded so that scientists can monitor the attraction and development of vegetation and animal life. It is possible to fly over the island but permission to land is rarely given.

Earthquakes, too, are common in Iceland although recently there have not been any as ferocious as those recorded in the eighteenth and nineteenth centuries. The most damaging occurred in the southern lowlands in 1784; in 1896 another destroyed many farms. The village of Dalvík in Eyjafjördur in the north was partly destroyed by an earthquake in 1934. Earthquakes have also been recorded around Krafla after its eruptions which have taken place every year since 1975. Unfortunately the volcanic and earthquake activity started shortly after work began on the country's first geothermal power station designed to trap the natural heat deep under the surface. Although completed for some years, the power station is now only working at maximum capacity of 30 megawatts because of the subterranean activity.

The last serious earthquake occurred in 1976 in the north-east when a number of tremors caused damage in the fishing village of Kópasker.

Iceland is also known for its geysers and hot springs. There are two types of hot spring, the *hver* which is a water or steam spring up to 100°C (212°F), and a *laug* where the water is only warm or lukewarm. Hot springs are very common in the volcanic areas although the *laug* also occurs in basalt formations. The Deildartunguhver in Borgarfjördur yields 250 litres (55 gallons) of boiling water every second and is probably the world's largest hot spring.

The Great, or Old, Geysir is the best known geyser, but in recent years it has spouted only seldom and irregularly. It used to be 'persuaded' to perform, however, by the warden of the area who threw large bars of soap down into its mouth although this has now been discouraged. The surface of the water starts to bubble more and more violently; the water shoots upwards suddenly and then, with a sound of rushing wind, the geyser sends its jet 15-18m (50-60ft) into the air. It has been known to hurl its waterspout 55m (180ft) into the air. It was this geyser which gave its name to all the others around the world.

Iceland is richer in hot springs, mud pools and steam holes than any other country on earth and it is a strange feeling to cross a glacier, with ice metres thick, only to encounter a near-boiling hot spring.

The main high temperature areas are Torfajökull, east of Hekla, and Grimsvötn, in the Vatnajökull glacier; and to a lesser extent Hengill, near Reykjavík, and Kerlingarfjöll, Námafjall, Kverkfjöll, and Krísuvík, south of the capital.

There are approximately 250 geothermal areas in Iceland with nearly 800 hot springs, with an average water temperature of 75°C (167°F). Only a tiny percentage of the springs and their geothermal energy has been tapped by the population but the total power available from the biggest area alone is said to be equivalent to 1,500 megawatts.

The Icelandic word for a glacier is *jökull.* They cover about 11½ per cent of the land, about 11,000sq km (4,228sq ft). Vatnajökull is the biggest glacier in the world, outside Greenland and Antarctica. South of it are massive sand and gravel plains, where the rivers formed by melting ice spread out in all directions, and are constantly changing course. Conditions here are identical with those prevailing in Jutland and North Germany during the last Ice Age. In the last few years the climate has become warmer; many of the glaciers are now retreating and some of the smaller ones have virtually disappeared. This warming marks the end of the last mini-Ice Age which lasted from about 1600-1900. Almost all types of glaciers can be found in Iceland, from the small cirque glaciers to extensive glacier caps.

There are other sizeable glaciers in the central highlands, such as Langjökull, 1,025sq km (395sq miles). On a good day one of the smaller glaciers, Snaefellsjökull, across the bay from Reykjavík can be seen.

Although it is possible to cross the glaciers great care needs to be taken because there are many crevices and avalanches which can be a real danger.

Iceland is criss-crossed by rivers which fall into two categories, glacial and clear water. The glacial rivers rushing down from the high ground are blue-grey in colour, carrying with them minerals and debris from the ice. The clear water rivers are red from lakes or rainfall and are sparkling clean. The water is safe to drink almost everywhere on the island. The longest river is the Thjórsá, in the south, which runs for 230km (143 miles). The second is in the north-east, the Jökulsá

Ice blackened by debris, Sólheimajökull

á Fjöllum, 206km (128 miles). Due to the constant upheaval of the land, there are many spectacular waterfalls; the most spectacular are Gullfoss, with a drop of 32m (105ft), Dettifoss 44m (144ft) and Skógarfoss 70m (200ft). Needless to say, the Icelandic word for waterfall is *foss*.

About 7 per cent of the total usable hydro-electric power in Iceland has been utilised; it has been estimated that if it were all to be harnessed it would provide up to 4,000 megawatts.

There are also many beautiful lakes in Iceland, the most famous of which, Myvatn, is also an internationally famous bird reserve. Many of the lakes are formed by subsidence, or by volcanic craters filling up, while others are created when lava flows dam rivers. Iceland's five biggest lakes are: Thingvallavatn, 83sq km (32sq miles); Thórisvatn, 68sq km (26sq miles); Lögurinn, 52sq km (20sq miles); Hóp, a lagoon lake covering 45sq km (17sq miles); and Myvatn, extending to 38sq km (14½sq miles).

Vegetation and Animal Life

When the Vikings arrived in Iceland the country was wooded between mountain and shore, according to Ari the Learned. These woods probably contained low-growing birches and willow, traces of which can still be seen today. Most of the woods were felled for fuel, however, and the introduction of sheep and the onset of cold weather prevented their regrowth in the Middle Ages. Volcanic eruptions with their gases, and the advance of the glaciers during the latest 300-year-long mini-Ice Age from 1600 also destroyed large tracts of woodland. Experiments have shown that birch and a number of species of fir can survive, providing that sheep can be kept away.

The largest birch wood is to be found in East Iceland at Hallormsstadarskógur and there is another in the north at Fnjóskárdalur. Small remains of old woodlands can be found in a number of other inaccessible places, especially along the rapid glacial rivers to the south of Vatnajökull. Large areas which were formerly covered with woods are now partially or completely devoid of vegetation, and consist mostly of stone or gravel. The soil has long since been blown away. Moss and grass are, however, more widespread in Iceland than in northern Scandinavia and Greenland.

Although large tracts of the highlands are quite bare of vegetation, fertile meadows are to be found in the lowlands between 500m and 700m (1,640-2,300ft) and even higher, and there are various plants and flowers on the slopes of the hills. Although there are about 740 species of vascular plants in Iceland, nearly 300 of these are dandelions and hawkweeds found in the highlands. Grasses and sedge are the commonest vascular plants, but beautifully flowered members of the pink, saxifrage, rose and daisy families are also common. The flora is of mixed but predominantly European origin.

Plants of special interest for Europeans are those found in Iceland but not in the British Isles or North Europe. The most common of these is the arctic fireweed or river beauty, a willowherb (*Epilobium latifolium*) with its purple flowers. It grows densely on gravelly riverbanks, in river gorges, or gravelly dried out river beds.

The broad-leaved willow (*Salix callicarpaea*) is to be found growing all over the country, as well in the lowlands as in the central highlands. The northern green orchid (*Limnorchis hyperborea*) has sweetly scented flowers, and is to be found on grassy slopes in the lowlands. Lyngbyes sedge (*Carex lyngbyei*) is a tall and beautiful sedge, often growing very densely and forming a broad zone of vegetation out from the shores of small lakes.

Another species of special interest is the marsh felwort (*Lomatogonium rotatum*) with fine blue flowers. It grows in bogs, especially near the coast; it is common in the northern part of Iceland and is also found in Arctic Russia.

In Northern Iceland there are some Arctic species not found elsewhere on the island, for instance alpine whitlow-grass (*Draba alpina*), the foliose saxifrage (*Saxifraga foliosa*), the mountain heath (*Phyllodoce coerulea*), the upright primrose (*Primula stricta*), and the arctic harebell (*Campanula uniflora*). One of the most interesting species in Iceland is the sword moss (*Bryoxiphium norvegicum*) which in spite of its name, is not from Norway. It is typically found at the Lake Kleifarvatn in Krísuvík, in south-west Iceland, only 25km (15½ miles) south of Reykjavík. It has a curious geographical distribution, it is found in north-east Greenland, in some regions of North America and also in Mexico and the Far East.

About 450 species of lichen and about 550 species of moss are found in Iceland. With very few exceptions the Icelandic lichen flora is of a Scandinavian character. One species, *Neuropogon sulphureus*, which is common in the Icelandic mountains about 600m (1,970ft) is only found on the islands in the Arctic Ocean, yet in the southern hemisphere it can be found on the Antarctic continent, and in some parts of the high Andes.

Flowers proliferate among the rocky outcrops: this was taken at Hafragilsfoss

Plants take root despite the seemingly inhospitable terrain

The largest area of woodlands is at Hallormsstadur, consisting mainly of birch and the tallest trees extending to about 10m (33ft) high. The rowan, aspen and tea-leaf willow can be found but these species are not widespread. In a few places the tree line reaches up to 600m (2,000ft), but it is generally between 300m and 400m (1,000 and 1,300ft).

The central highlands and the mountains are almost bare of vegetation above the 700m (2,300ft) level. Only scattered species of very hardy Arctic-alpine plants can survive here. In the lowlands too, there are large areas devoid of vegetation, mostly because of lava flows. It is interesting to study the flora taking a foothold in the crumbling lava of the older flows as it turns to soil. First moss establishes itself and this mixes with the lava sand to provide a base for dwarf shrubs and later for birch.

The best examples of this lava flow vegetation can be found in the Búdahraun and the Myvatn area. In these lava flows there are always ravines and in this sheltered environment an even more luxurious vegetation of ferns, herbs and grasses develops. The warm soil around the hot springs also provides favourable conditions for plants, and some species can only be found in such places in Iceland.

Iceland is at the crossroads of several migration routes, so in addition to its resident bird population, it gets visitors from all points of the compass. It is the westernmost outpost of a number of Old World species and the easternmost of some New World ones. In all some 240 species of birds have been seen in Iceland at one time or another, and of these eighty nest in the country. There are seven common passage migrants or winter visitors and a number of regular drift visitors; the remainder are accidentals brought in by freak weather. A great attraction for bird watchers is the tameness of the birds. One reason for this is the small size of the human population compared to the size of the country, some 240,000 people in a 103,600sq km (40,000sq mile) area. Iceland's most famous bird is the Iceland falcon which is now fully protected. It is still widely distributed in the rocky and mountainous parts of the country and is a wonder to watch as it swoops through the air. The white-tailed eagle, once common, is now rare and there are serious fears about its chances of survival. There are only about ten breeding pairs left, mostly in the Breidafjördur area in the west and the mountainous north-west peninsula. The small merlin is the third bird of prey to be found in Iceland.

Two species of owl can be found, the magnificent snowy owl, which is very rare and restricted to certain wild parts of the central highlands, and the short-eared owl, found in low-lying moorland and valleys. The short-eared owl is one of nine species which have settled and bred in the country during the gradual warming of the climate in the last few decades. This owl feeds on mice and small birds, while the snowy owl, like the falcon, usually preys on the ptarmigan, which is the country's most important game bird. There are only nine nesting passerines, mostly because of lack of suitable habitats, especially the absence of real woods, and to the scarcity of insect life.

Iceland has an international reputation as one of the major breeding grounds for waterfowl in Europe, and Myvatn is the home in the summer for tens of thousands of birds. This shallow lake supports Europe's and perhaps the world's, largest concentration of breeding duck. On the lake and surrounding rivers all seventeen species of duck which nest in Iceland can be found; sometimes more than 150,000 duck are assembled on the waters and lake shore.

Two American representatives of the duck tribe, the Barrow's goldeneye and the harlequin, nest here. The Barrow's goldeneye only nests at Myvatn while the harlequin breeds throughout the island. The scaup is the lake's most abundant duck but other species to be found are the tufted duck, common scoter, and long-tailed duck. The common pochard is a new immigrant and still rare.

There are two nesting species of geese in Iceland and passage migrants. The greylag goose inhabits the low-lying district, while the pink-footed goose inhabits the central highlands. The white-fronted goose, brent goose and barnacle goose are visitors. The eider is the island's most common duck and there are more than 200 breeding colonies.

The whooper swan is a common breeding bird, and Iceland is one of the few places in Europe where this is so. It is most numerous on the lakes of the central highlands.

There are still huge colonies of breeding sea birds around Iceland, and the most common species are the common guillemot, Brünnich's guillemot, the puffin, the razor-bill, the kittiwake and the fulmar. The puffin does not only breed on the cliffs; huge colonies can be found on low-lying grassy islands. It is one of the commonest Icelandic birds with a population running into millions. Both the birds and eggs are eaten by the people living on the Vestmannaeyjar.

The taking of birds and eggs is a centuries-old tradition and used to be a valuable source of food. In the middle of the last century, records show that tens of thousands of fledglings were taken from the nests each year. By the turn of the century more than 50,000 fledglings were being taken annually from the huge fulmar colonies on Grímsey. The meat was eaten then, or salted or dried for the winter, the feathers were used for bedding and the rest was melted down for oil for the lamps.

Iceland is one of the few places where the ranges of the common and Brünnich's guillemot overlap, and the two species nest in mixed colonies. Two other members of the auk family are the black guillemot, which nests in small colonies among boulders on rocky coasts and islands, and the little auk, a high Arctic species which is now practically extinct.

The Westman Islands (Vestmannaeyjar) are an excellent place to study birds; three species of the petrel family can be found there; the Manx shearwater, Leach's petrel and the storm petrel, which are not found anywhere else in Iceland. There are also gannet colonies on four of the outlying islands, although the largest is on Eldey, off the south-west coast. There are about 15,000 pairs of gannets nesting

Aldeyjarfoss
Dramatic waterfalls like this
occur all over Iceland

in this isolated rock. The cormorant and the shag are both common and most abundant in the bays of the west coast, Faxaflói and the Breidafjördur.

Despite its name the Iceland gull does not nest in Iceland but in west Greenland although it is a common winter visitor. The arctic tern is the only tern to be found and it is abundant; and the skuas are represented by the arctic skua and the great skua. The former is common while the latter inhabits the glacial outwash plains in the south-eastern and southern parts of the country. Only the arctic or blue fox is native to Iceland. Mice and rats came ashore with the settlers, and reindeers now live wild in the western highlands. There are no reptiles or amphibians in Iceland.

There are strict laws governing the photographing and visiting of sites of rare birds, especially eagles, falcons, snowy owls and little auks. Permits are only issued by the Ministry of Education following a recommendation from the Bird Protection Committee, and there are heavy fines for breaking these laws.

The farmers mostly raise sheep, which was until 1914 the main occupation. For most of the summer the sheep are grazed on the extensive meadow and heathland pastures, often far up into the mountains. The flocks are rounded up for slaughter in the autumn before the first of the heavy snows. The breeding ewes are kept indoors throughout the winter as are cattle. The breeds of sheep, cattle and horses are all indigenous, derived from Nordic origin. Dairy and sheep farming are the most important enterprises in all parts of the country and beef production is of relatively little importance. Wool is an important by-product of sheep farming. There are about three-quarters of a million sheep on the island and about 60,000 cattle.

Modern farming techniques, machinery and drainage equipment is allowing more arable land to be created. Four hundred years ago cereals were grown, but the onset of much colder weather put an end to this. Today the main crop is still hay to feed the animals during the long winter months, but more land is constantly being recovered for cropping.

The People and Industry

The people of Iceland are mainly of a mixed Scandinavian and Celtic stock. The first settlers were Norwegian, and the language and culture have always been Scandinavian, although there are Celtic influences brought in by the Irish colonists.

CODE FOR VISITORS

1 Please respect the signs of the Nature Conservation Council and the Public Roads Administration traffic and other signs.
2 Driving off roads and tracks is prohibited.
3 It is forbidden to damage or destroy vegetation.
4 Gathering firewood and lighting fires on or near vegetation is prohibited.
5 Where there is no vegetation, fires may be lighted, care being taken not to cause any danger and to leave no marks.
6 Those who travel in the open countryside shall take care not to leave behind refuse. All refuse should be deposited in proper refuse containers.
7 It is prohibited to make marks on natural features.
8 It is prohibited to spoil hot springs and pools, eg by throwing rocks or other objects into them or by damaging the sinter surrounding the springs.
9 Export of birds, eggs, egg shells and nests is unlawful.
10 In protected areas there are special rules. Only the Nature Conservation Council can allow exemptions from these rules:
Activities which alter the landscape or living nature are prohibited.
Collection of natural objects such as animals, plants and rocks is forbidden.
Camping is limited to designated campsites in or close to inhabited areas and is excluded in National Parks and areas of Scientific Interest.

The Sagas are one of the world's richest literary collections. They were written down mostly in the thirteenth century and were a detailed account of the settlement of Iceland and its subsequent history. They give a graphic account of life, customs, superstitions, and are an essential read if you really want to understand the nature of the Icelandic people.

The Icelanders are so proud of their heritage, and so anxious to preserve it, that they have passed a law which stipulates that it is illegal to give a child a non-Icelandic name.

Less than 20 per cent of the population now live in rural areas, and a third of the people live in and around Reykjavík. For 800 years almost all the population lived in the countryside, but at the turn of this century, the migration to the towns began, helped largely by the dawning of industrialisation. The rural inhabitants live mostly on the 5,000 or so farms.

Many Icelandic roads, including many major roads, are not surfaced. This is part of the main circular route around Iceland leading to Grímsstadir, close to Mödrudalur farm, the highest in Iceland.

Living on the farms used to be a hard life. The summers were short and filled with hard work although food was plentiful. The winters were long and dark, times for the family to be together, times of shortages. Much of the land is unproductive and so farming is not a major economic factor. Although the roots of the country lie in the rural areas (it was on the farms and in the country monasteries that the Sagas were written), the emphasis has now switched to the towns. In 1880 there were only three towns in Iceland where 5 per cent of the population lived; but now there are nineteen towns and thirty-eight villages where 86.9 per cent of the population live. Iceland is the most sparsely populated country in Europe, with an average of two inhabitants per square kilometre.

Greenhouses heated with hot water and steam from deep in the earth provide salad crops and fruit, even bananas. The first green-house to be heated in this way opened in 1924 and there is now a large complex of glass, east of Reykjavík.

The major industry, however, is fishing, accounting for 70 per cent of the country's exports. Although it occupies only 5 per cent of the population, it provides more than 10,000 jobs in canning and associated industries. Cod and haddock are the most important species, although prawns and lobsters are a lucrative catch. Fish farming is becoming important and there is still some whaling for scientific research and sealing although the former is likely to be phased out, and the island's only whaling station, to the north of Reykjavík is probably going to stay open as a tourist attraction preserved as a museum to the industry. There has been much concern due to overfishing, culminating in the 'Cod Wars' of the 1970s, when restrictions where increased to 200 miles.

Industry is a relatively new development in Iceland although there have always been cottage and farmhouse industries producing the famous Icelandic knitwear, and other crafts. Industry now, however, employs more people than farming and fishing together although their basic product is still fish and agricultural produce. The largest industrial plant is at Straumsvík, to the east of Reykjavík; a Swiss-owned aluminium reduction factory which imports ore from Australia. The huge red and white smelter towers are visible for miles. The island has its own cement and nitrogen fertilizer plants and the machine and building industries are growing in importance. There is a diatromite plant near Myvatn which produces filtering agents for the brewing and chemical industries from the processed skeletons of minute creatures that form a thick layer on the bottom of the lake.

Iceland is fortunate in having virtually unlimited supplies of energy and electricity simply by tapping into geothermal wells, or building hydro-electric stations on the cascading rivers and waterfalls.

Iceland is now rapidly developing a reputation as a conference venue and facilities are available in Reykjavík to hold international meetings. The country has recently played host to two such meetings which focused world attention on them. It was the venue of the world chess championships in the 1970s, and more recently, and more momentously was the venue for the Reagan-Gorbachev summit.

Travel Information

Icelandair flies regularly to the international airport at Keflavík from a number of European and North American cities. Scandinavian Airlines (SAS) flies from Copenhagen to Iceland, and there are also flights from Oslo and Stockholm operated on a pooled basis with Icelandair. Connecting flights are available from a number of major cities. In addition to normal one-way and return fares a number of other excursion and family fares are available, and there are also special group rates.

One of the best ways of travelling to Iceland and seeing the country is to go on an arranged package holiday and several of these are now available. Flying in to the international airport at Keflavík can be one of the highlights of the trip if the weather is fine. As you begin your descent the flight path normally takes you over the Westman Islands and you should be able to see mountains and glaciers running down to the southern coast. Keflavík, with its new terminal buildings, is unique in Europe in that you can enter the duty free shop and purchase alcohol on arrival as well as departure.

There is a bank at the airport which will change foreign currency and travellers cheques, and a tourist information desk. Cars can be hired at the airport, although it speeds things up if these have been booked in advance, and there are taxis and buses to take you into Reykjavík. The buses normally drop passengers at the Loftleidir Hotel in Reykjavík. The 48km (30 mile) journey takes about 40-50 minutes depending on the time of day.

Passengers must re-confirm their return flights at least 24 hours before departure. Buses leave the Loftleidir Hotel to give you plenty of time to check in and bus tickets can be bought from the desk in the hotel foyer.

Bare rock accounts for approximately 10 per cent of the landscape

Because of the distances involved, and the state of the roads, flying is the most popular way of internal travel. Almost every community has its own small airstrip, although it is difficult when looking at some of them to see just how the aircraft land there. There are three main air operators — Icelandair (Flugleidir), and its two subsidiaries Flugfélag Nordurlands, which operates out of Akureyri, and Flugfélag Austurlands, operating from Egilsstadir. These airlines operate throughout the year and are heavily relied on during the winter when many of the roads are impassable. Because the weather can change so quickly, it is always advisable to check in advance that a scheduled flight is running, and you must be prepared to face delays on occasions.

There are scheduled services from Reykjavík to Akureyri (6-7 flights daily), Bakkafjördur, Bíldudalur, Borgarfjördur, Breiddalsvík, Egilsstadir, Fáskrúdsfjördur, Flateyri, Grímsey, Hornafjördur, Húsavík, Ingjaldssandur, Ísafjördur, Nordfjördur, Ólafsfjördur, Patreksfjördur, Raufarhöfn, Reykjanes, Saudárkrókur, Siglufjördur, Sudureyri, Thingeyri, Thórshöfn, Vestmannaeyjar and Vopnafjördur.

From Ísafjördur there are flights to Bíldudalur, Flateyri,

Ingjaldssandur, Patreksfjördur, Reykjanes, Sudureyri and Thingeyri.

From Akureyri there are flights to Egilsstadir, Grímsey, Húsavík, Ísafjördur, Kópasker, Ólafsfjördur, Raufarhöfn, Siglufjördur, Thórshöfn and Vopnafjördur.

From Egilsstadir there are flights to Bakkafjördur, Borgarfjördur, Breiddalsvík, Fáskrúdsfjördur, Hornafjördur, Nordfjördur, Reykjavík and Vopnafjördur. There are also flights from Breiddalsvík, Fáskrúdsfjördur and Nordfjördur to Reykjavík.

Apart from the normal fares there is a number of special packages including: family fares — only one adult pays the normal fare, the other adult and children aged between 12 and 20, are entitled to a 50 per cent discount, and children aged between 2 and 11 pay half the regular children's fares.

Standby fares are available on a number of flights affording big savings, and groups, senior citizens and students are also entitled to discounts. Many of these flights are met by bus services so that you can continue your journey, and a number of airports have taxis, or facilities to call them. If you have a long journey to make on arrival, it is a good idea to book your taxi in advance.

The only ferry service to Iceland is via the Faroes. Smyril Line of Tórshavn operates a weekly passenger and car ferry service between the Faroe Islands and Seydisfjördur on the eastern coast of Iceland, as well as to Lerwick, in Shetland, to Bergen in Norway and to Hantsholm in Denmark. If you want to bring your own vehicle in from the UK, you will have to get to Lerwick in Shetland and there catch the ferry for Tórshavn in the Faroes. If you are bringing your own car into Iceland you must have the log book, green card and a current driving licence. Mud flaps must be fitted to stop stones being thrown up.

Maximum dimensions for vehicles allowed is width 2.5m (8.2ft) and length 13m (42.6ft). Vehicles which carry fifteen or more passengers are not allowed to have trailers, and fuel can only be imported in a vehicle's tank, empty spare cans can be brought in and filled on the island.

The ferry lands at Seydisfjördur, one of the prettiest settlements on the east coast, and you then have a spectacular car journey to make over the mountains to Egilsstadir, the main town of the region. Buses also meet the ferry to take passengers to Egilsstadir.

For drivers arriving in Iceland for the first time, the road out of the port and up the hairpin bends is a good introduction to island driving.

Stop somewhere safe as you climb out of the valley and take in the spectacular views of the port nestling in its fjord, and the plunging cliffs with scores of waterfalls as the backdrop.

The Iceland Steamship Company maintains a regular freighter service from many ports in Northern Europe and the USA to Iceland, and special passenger rates can be arranged.

A valid passport is necessary for travellers coming to Iceland, except those of Danish, Faroese, Finnish, Norwegian and Swedish nationalities. British citizens do not need a visa; nor do citizens of most western European countries, British Commonwealth or America.

The Icelandic monetary unit is the *krona* which is equal to 100 *aurar*. There are 1kr, 5kr, 10kr, 50 aurar and 5 aurar coins, and banknotes are 10kr, 50kr, 100kr, 500kr and 1,000kr. Travellers are allowed to bring in any amount of foreign currency in letters of credit, travellers' cheques, or banknotes which can be easily cashed into *krónur*. You must not take notes of higher than 100kr out of the country. Most large hotels will change foreign currency or travellers' cheques, as will restaurants and department stores. The major credit cards are also widely accepted. It is possible to cash unused *krónur* but only if you have the original exchange note with you. Banks are open for business from Mondays to Fridays between 9.15am and 4pm.

Car ferries ply between Reykjavík and Akranes, sailing across Faxaflói and there is a larger ferry sailing from Thorlákshöfn on the south coast to the Westman Islands. In the west a ferry operates between Stykkishólmur carrying both cars and passengers to Brjánslaekur, via the Breidafjördur Islands, while another sails between a number of ports along the Ísafjardardjúp. There are regular sailings from Akureyri to the island of Grímsey. There is also a ferry service to the island of Hrísey in Eyjafjördur.

It can be quite exciting driving in Iceland because the roads vary from good in the south to almost impassable inland. Vehicles drive on the right. Drink-driving laws are very strict. It is worth remembering that it is little more than 15 years since the road around the island was completed. In 1974, to commemorate the 1,000th anniversary of the first settlement, the final stretch of the coastal ring road was completed when the section below the Vatnajökull glacier was opened. This elevated roadway was a remarkable piece of engineering, because year after year, flood waters from the thawing snow came down from the mountains and glaciers, sweeping away the roads and bridges in their path. The completion of that road means that it is now possible to travel completely around the island and it can be a rewarding, if somewhat bumpy experience.

One must keep to roads that are marked on the maps. There are plenty of tracks to follow but many of these are made by farmers or people who know the area thoroughly and the stranger straying onto these is likely to get lost. Sandstorms and fog often cause unexpected problems, with reduced visibility, and caution should always be exercised when crossing fords. The water is very clear and therefore may be deceptively deep. Glacial rivers are also very dangerous to cross even in four-wheel drive vehicles. The currents are usually very strong and large boulders can easily be swept along by them.

Because there are large stretches of uninhabited countryside, there are rescue huts for passengers in emergencies. They are not meant to accommodate the ordinary traveller, and provisions and first aid equipment should never be touched unless urgently needed.

Traffic in Iceland gives way to the left. International signs are used and there is adequate signposting on most of the main roads.

One of the best ways to see the island, and one of the cheapest, is to travel by coach. There are frequent excursions and tours leaving from Reykjavík, Akureyri and other towns, as well as a remarkable island bus service. It is possible, over a few days, to do the round trip using scheduled coach services staying on campsites, hostels or cheap hotels overnight. It is also a very good way of meeting the people of Iceland, because their natural friendliness will almost always lead to conversation. The coaches normally leave early in the morning and can be on the road for up to 12 hours, but they stop regularly for comfort and refreshment breaks. In both Reykjavík and Akureyri there are also inter-town bus services.

Iceland buses are like no others, and when you see the roads they have to travel over, you can understand why. Most of the buses are specially built, with higher than usual clearance, because of boulders and pot holes, four-wheel drive and two way radios so that the driver can keep in touch with base.

BSI, the Icelandic Bus Routes Union, operates most of the scheduled services although it and a number of small companies also run tours. During the summer months, the buses run into the interior, and this is one of the best ways to explore, letting the driver do the hard work while you enjoy the scenery.

If you plan to use the buses to travel around the island, there are a number of special discount tickets available. An Omnibus Passport can last from 1 to 4 weeks and allows you to use all the scheduled routes, apart from the interior ones. You can get off where you like, spend some days walking or exploring before continuing the journey. There is also the Full-Circle Passport which allows you to travel the ring road, but once you have decided which way you are going, you must continue your trip in that direction. You are still allowed to break your journey when and as often as you like.

If you plan to travel the island by bus, get hold of a copy of the BSI time-table. Although only available in Icelandic, it is understandable and will allow you to work out a route using the forty or so scheduled services which cover almost 4,000km (2,480 miles) of roads.

There are many taxis in the principal towns. There is no tipping in Iceland. Taxis can also be hired at a fairly reasonable rate for extended trips into the country.

Car hire is expensive, especially if you want a four-wheel drive vehicle, but an all-terrain vehicle is absolutely essential if you plan to get off the main routes and use mountain roads. It is a good idea to have an international driving licence, but it is not essential.

When you pick up your hire vehicle, check it out carefully. Make sure the tyres are in good condition, that the spare tyre is usable, and that you know where the jack and tools are. Often the vehicles come without any English manuals so make sure you know the basics before you set out. If you are planning to go into the remote areas, make sure you have a good tool kit and spares, and if you plan to drive along some of the more dangerous mountain roads, go in convoy with at least one other vehicle.

Icelandair Car Rental will provide a map showing all the garages around the island which will help out if you have a problem, but all these are located on or near the ring road. Once you head into the interior, you are very much on your own, although there may be isolated farms where you can get help or fuel. All types of cars can be rented for use, either on a daily or weekly basis. Vehicles are only rented to people over 20 years of age. The rate is normally calculated on a daily hire charge plus mileage. Fuel and 25 per cent sales tax are not included.

The Iceland Tourist Board issues a number of useful leaflets for visiting drivers. It would be a good idea if 'How to Travel in the Interior of Iceland', and 'Some Things You Must Know', were automatically handed over to vehicle hirers.

It is essential when travelling to have good maps and there are large scale charts available of most areas. There is also a very good road atlas published by Landmaelingar Islands, which is ideal for motorists and planning routes.

Don't get confused by road signs. Often when you are moving off a main road, the signpost will not indicate the number of the road you are about to drive on, but the road it connects with.

Some stretches of roads in built up areas have paved surfaces and there are even occasional stretches of dual carriageway, but these are not really needed. There are traffic jams in the cities during the rush hours, but generally the roads are quiet.

The major roads in the south, especially those from the international airport at Keflavík leading into Reykjavík, and those to the other towns in the south-east and south have asphalt surfaces. Most other roads are of graded gravel and while in the summer all roads are open, great care should be taken before venturing too far off the beaten track. To do any serious travelling in the hinterland, a four-wheel drive vehicle is necessary, and it is much safer to travel in pairs so that one vehicle can be on hand to pull the other out of trouble if necessary.

There were no roads in Iceland before 1900 and when the tracks were created they were primarily for pack horses. In fact, until quite recently horses were used as the main method of carrying goods, provisions and materials inland. There have never been any railways on the island.

There are now about 11,000km (6,800 miles) of roads, although more than 20 per cent of these are country roads linking farms and rural settlements. There has also been an intensive bridge building programme and now all the main rivers are crossable by bridge rather than having to find a suitable fording place as used to be the case some years ago.

There are a number of rules which have to be followed if you are planning to go off inland by yourself. Never drive on vegetation off the road. There is little enough of it about in Iceland and it takes a long time to recover. It could also lead to soil erosion. The mountain roads and tracks are only passable using four-wheel drive vehicles.

For touring in summer, lightweight woollens are necessary, a sweater or cardigan for the evening, as well as waterproofs and sturdy footwear. Swimming gear is essential whenever you are travelling because there are numerous hot pools, warm springs and heated swimming pools.

A winter visit will require warmer clothing, but the temperature is rarely as cold as in Scotland and northern England, and warm jumpers and stout overcoats are more than sufficient.

The best hotels are in Reykjavík but there are many first-class establishments to be found elsewhere in Iceland, especially in the north. The top hotels are of international standard, although there are many others to suit all budgets. In the summer, many of the schools in the country have 3 months' holiday and these buildings are converted into 'summer hotels' for travellers. The basic facilities of bed, washrooms and kitchens are provided, and you have the choice of eating a prepared meal or catering for yourself. There are also guesthouses available in most towns, and many private houses offer bed and breakfast accommodation, especially in Reykjavík. It is also now possible to stay on farms in Iceland and terms include both room only and full board. There is no tipping in Icelandic hotels, breakfast is never included in the price of the room, although most hotels have their own restaurants offering a full meals service.

There are many camping sites in Iceland. There is a large site in Reykjavík near the main bus terminal, and another in the city centre, next to the magnificent swimming pool. Some sites are well appointed with showers and toilets, although in some of the remoter areas naturally there are fewer facilities. Most communities have a municipal camping site just outside the town, and camping is generally permitted anywhere in Iceland, unless there are signs specifically forbidding it. Camping is not allowed inside the country's three national parks, nor in areas of special scientific interest, although notices are not generally on display. One can normally camp near farms or fenced land, but one should obtain prior permission from the farmer.

There are many youth hostels in Iceland and a new one is nearing completion in Reykjavík. Many country hotels also offer special reduced priced accommodation for travellers who provide their own sleeping bags. In the hinterland, there are a number of huts owned by the Icelandic Touring Club. It is normally best to check if these are available as they are frequently used by large groups. In these huts one must provide one's own sleeping bag and food. Groups travelling with the club always have priority.

There has been quite an upsurge in catering standards in Iceland in the last few years, although the top hotels have always offered an international cuisine of a high standard. In Reykjavík there are now many small establishments offering excellent varied food, such as salmon, raw shark, sheep's head and Icelandic blue cheese. Needless to say, the fish restaurants are excellent but there are also now American burger bars and a host of other foreign cuisines. It must be said that eating out is not cheap, although standards are high. Because breakfast is not always included in the hotel's overnight charge, it is often better to eat out and there are many restaurants and cafés offering budget breakfasts.

Most hotels and restaurants have licences to serve spirits and wines but until recently strong beer was almost unobtainable — a remnant of the prohibition laws. Until last year, the only beer generally available was low-alcohol or non-alcoholic beer. The Government has now decided that normal strength beer can be sold. There are, however, some restaurants which are 'dry' and only soft drinks are available.

It is worth mentioning that Iceland is one of the few countries in the world where you can buy your duty free drinks as you go into the country. Tourists can bring into Iceland, tax free, one litre of wine or other drinks (up to 21 per cent alcohol), or twelve bottles of beer, as well as one litre of spirits, and 200 cigarettes or equivalent of other tobacco products.

There are discos in both Reykjavík and Akureyri, and the Broadway, in the capital, claims to be the largest disco in Europe. Friday and Saturday are the most popular nights. Icelanders are very fond of dancing, and most communities organise their own dances to which tourists are made welcome. These may not be held regularly but they are always well advertised.

All musical tastes are catered for in Reykjavík and apart from ballroom dances at some of the hotels, and the discos, there are classical concerts, jazz clubs and folk clubs. There are nine cinemas in Reykjavík alone, and all towns of any size have their own cinema. Films are normally shown in their original language with Icelandic subtitles, and releases tend to be up to date. Normally only a main feature is shown.

During the summer months in Reykjavík there is a presentation of traditional Icelandic folklore, with songs, dances and Saga readings. Performances are held several times a week between early July and the end of August. The performances are normally in English. The Icelandic Opera also presents a series of musical evenings in July and August, although the National Theatre and Municipal Theatre are closed in the summer.

The Society of Icelandic Solo Singers gives recitals of Icelandic poetry and songs every week in July and August and Icelandic documentary films are screened daily during the summer in Reykjavík.

Shops are open weekdays from 9am to 6pm and on Saturdays from 9am or 10am to noon, although many close for the whole weekend. Offices are open 9am to 5pm weekdays only, and few work on Saturdays. Shops offer the normal range of goods and there are many gift and souvenir shops. Favourite souvenirs are sheepskins, woollen goods, jewellery, and lava pottery. Icelandic wool is especially soft yet strong, and much of the knitwear is handmade.

Almost every sort of sporting facility can be found. Swimming is the most popular activity and there are heated pools in all large towns. Because the water is heated from geothermal wells, swimming is an all-year-round activity, even if the air temperature is at freezing point or below. Most of the swimming pools also have 'hot pots'. These are pools which tap straight into the hot water reservoirs underground and their temperatures vary from very hot to scalding, yet some locals seem to able to immerse themselves in the hottest pools for long periods. Saunas and sulphur pools are also common throughout the island.

There are a number of good golf courses around the country and golf is now a very popular pastime with the Icelanders. For the last few years a very successful international tournament — the Arctic Open — has been held at the Akureyri Golf Club. The tournament is always played in mid-summer on what is proudly claimed to be the most northerly 18-hole course in the world. A growing number of foreign golfers are flying in specially for the tournament although they do have a slight handicap — at least to start with. As it is the land of the midnight sun, the competitors normally tee off at midnight and finish their rounds in the early hours of the morning.

Horse riding and pony trekking is now becoming a very popular activity. Fishing is popular with both locals and visitors alike, and there is some of the best salmon and trout fishing in Europe to be had in the Icelandic streams. Licences are needed to fish all fresh water streams and rivers, and booking well in advance is necessary for the best stretches. Because there are no fish diseases in Iceland all fishing gear brought into the country must be sterilised. Apart from trout and salmon, there is fishing for char, and fishing lodges providing excellent holidays are now being established. Skiing is available in many areas, especially in the north.

In all hotels, the receptionist will summon medical aid if you request it. Britain has a reciprocal health agreement with Iceland but medical insurance is advisable.

The national religion is Lutheran but there is complete freedom of worship. About 2 per cent of the population is Roman Catholic, and Reykjavík has a Roman Catholic cathedral. Two final pieces of general information: the electricity supply is 220 volts 50Hz AC, while Reykjavík is permanently on Greenwich Mean Time (GMT).

Fishing in Iceland

Iceland has some of the best and cheapest salmon and trout fishing in the world. It has one of the few capital cities (possibly the only one), where salmon can be caught in the town; and in places, especially off the north coast, fishing is free.

While Iceland has always been popular with fishermen because of the good sport, attempts are now being made to increase facilities. Fishing lodges are being built alongside the best stretches of water, and an excellent one has now been built to the north of Reykjavík on the Laxá (Stóra Laxá) river.

Iceland has three species of sports fish generally distributed — the salmon, brown trout and char. In addition there is the stickleback and the common eel. Two other species of trout can also be caught, but both are 'imports'. Rainbow trout were originally introduced from Denmark and are now bred on fish farms for stocking lakes and rivers. They are also farmed commercially. A few pink salmon have also been caught, and these are believed to be descendants from North Russian stock which have migrated. Both of the last two species have been fished for the last 25 years.

Salmon always return to the river in which they were born to spawn, so salmon found in Iceland are truly Icelandic fish. The salmon's huge areas of travel have led to serious problems of conservation in the last few years. Overfishing in one area can lead to serious depletion of stock returning to spawn in another. International agreements have now been signed which should help reduce overall salmon catches and help the species increase again. In 1984, however, 23,582 salmon were caught by use of a rod or line.

In Iceland, almost all the salmon is caught inland, in rivers and lakes. In most cases fishing for salmon at sea is banned by law, even though many other countries permit this. Because the salmon is caught inshore, it is classified as freshwater fish, as are the brown trout and char. Often the trout and char go to the sea to feed, and sea trout and sea char provide excellent fishing as they grow bigger and faster.

Iceland has at least sixty rivers with salmon, and many more with trout. The salmon can be found anywhere along the river's length from a few kilometres to more than 100km (60 miles) inland. The island's best salmon fishing is to be found in the south-west, in the rivers around Reykjavík, and two-thirds of the catch is taken in this region. The best rivers are the Ölfusá-Hvítá complex, Sog, Brúará and Stóra Laxá in Arnesysla. In the Borgarfjördur valley there is another Hvítá river system with its main tributaries of Grímsá, Thverá and Nordurá.

The river Ellidaár runs through Reykjavík, and this is probably the country's most famous salmon river, with one of the highest yields. Another good stretch of water is to be found north of Reykjavík on the river Laxá in Kjós.

In the north-west of the country there are many good stretches of river around the Dalasysla district. The Húnavatnssyla area also has many good waters including Midfjardará, the Laxá, Blandá and Vatnsdalsá. The best salmon river in the north-east is the Laxá which flows majestically, with many deep pools and islands, from the town of Húsavík. Other good waters are to be found in the Thistilfjördur and Vopnafjördur districts.

There is not much salmon fishing in the south-east, although there have been catches. Most of the rivers are glacial, and therefore short, although they do contain sea trout. Sea trout weighing up to 20lb are not uncommon in the Skaftá to the west of the Vatnajökull glacier.

Trout can be fished almost anywhere on the island's coastal plains, but the best areas are in the south-east and south-west. Sea char is most common in the north-west, north-east and south-west, and is the main fish of the short, fast flowing rivers of the north-west peninsula.

There is also good lake fishing and offshore fishing. Lake trout of up to 26lb are not unusual, but lake char is the commonest fish. In the south-west there are about twenty first class fishing lakes, of which Thingvallavatn is the largest. It is about 40km (25 miles) east of the capital. Other good lakes are Apavatn, east of Thingvallavatn; Hlídarvatn and Kleifarvatn, south of Reykjavík; and Hvalvatn, Reydarvatn, Langavatn, Hítarvatn and Oddastadavatn.

The Húnavatnssyla district, in the north-west, also has many fine fishing lakes. Hóp is the country's fourth largest lake, and there are also the lakes of Vesturhópsavtn, Svínavatn, and Laxárvatn.

Lake Myvatn dominates the fishing in the north-east. It is the country's fifth largest lake, and being able to hire a boat, and row out into the middle of this beautiful lake, is a wonderful experience, even if you don't catch anything. The views make it worthwhile.

The south-west, because of its glacial, heavily mineralised waters, has a number of lakes which cannot support fish life. The country's second largest lake, Thórisvatn, is to be found here, but it has no fish. Some brown trout can be found to the south in the group of lakes known as Veidivötn.

The Icelandic salmon varies between 4lb and 12lb and between 55cm and 85cm (21in and 33in) in length. Every year, fish approaching 30lb are caught, and the record is a 49lb fish (after bleeding) which was caught in a cod net off the island of Grímsey in 1957. It was 132cm (52in) long. The largest rod-caught salmon was taken in 1946 at Ida in the Hvítá river in Árnessysla. It weighed 38½lb.

Sea trout can weight up to 20lb, though most weigh between 1lb and 4lb. Sea char are usually smaller, weighing in at between 1lb and 2lb, although some of 12lb have been taken.

The lake brown trout usually grow up to 4lb, although a giant one weighing 26lb was caught at Thingvallavatn. Lake char is the commonest species in the lakes and can vary enormously in size, from anything from 3 or 4oz to 12lb. The average weight is between ½lb and 2lb.

In Thingvallavatn, a special variety of char can be found. It grows to about 20cm (8in) in length and weighs about 4oz.

Salmon may only be fished for 4 months of the year, from 20 May to 20 September. Net fishing starts on 20 May, but generally rod fishing is not allowed until June, and the date varies according to the area. In the north, because the rivers are colder, the fish do not travel up the rivers until July and this is generally considered the best fishing month. August is usually good, and in some years exceptional, while in September, the sport is beginning to decline.

Cod's heads drying in the sun. These are exported to such places as Nigeria as they are a valuable source of protein.

The sea trout season opens on 1 April and closes on 20 September. The best early fishing is in the south as the trout make their way to sea. The main fishing season, however, is in July and August as the fish return to the rivers to spawn. Fishing in the lakes is allowed from 1 February to 26 September, except at Thingvallavatn, where the season closes on 31 August. The best fishing is from late May until the middle of July.

The traditional methods of winter fishing through the ice are still practised in some areas, although this is a very chilly way of catching your supper. Fishing rights are held by the landowner. Many owners have formed themselves into associations to control the fishing. The fishing is often rented out on a yearly basis to clubs or individuals, who allocate rights. The right to fish is usually granted from 1 to 3 days, and because of the excellence of the fishing the finest stretches are booked up months, sometimes years ahead. Fishing is controlled to protect the stock, and limits are imposed on the numbers of rods allowed on each stretch. This means that a fisherman can be given a stretch of river several hundred metres, or even kilometres long, so there is no shortage of places to cast from.

Fishing is allowed for 12 hours a day, from 7am to 10pm with a 2 or 3 hour break for lunch. The fisherman is usually allowed to keep all his catch. Trout fishing permits can normally be obtained on the day by applying direct to the farmer, or through his agent, who is usually to be found in the nearest town or hotel.

Most Icelanders prefer to use a rod for fishing, and although netting is allowed in some areas it is becoming less popular. Fly rods of 2.7 to 4.2m (9 to 14ft), and casting rods of about 2.7m (9ft) are preferred for salmon using bait of earthworm, artificial fly, spinner or lure. The most popular artificial flies are: Black Doctor, Blue Charm, Crossfield, Silver Doctor, Silver Wilkinson and Silver Grey. Similar baits are used for trout.

The larger fishing lodges provide food and bedding, although self-catering is available in some. The smaller lodges have basic facilities and fishermen must fend for themselves. Many hotels now offer fishing package holidays, if there are good waters nearby.

For health reasons the use of fishing equipment, including waders and rubber boots, which have been used while angling abroad is prohibited, unless it has been disinfected according to the rules.

Riding in Iceland

For hundreds of years the Icelandic horse (for horse it is despite its small size), has been the most useful animal on the island. It has been the pack horse, and until recently, the only means of transport in many parts of the country. It is still used by farmers each year to round up the tens of thousands of sheep grazing on the lowland plains.

In common with horses in many other parts of the world, the animal has generally fallen into disuse as a working beast, and is now kept mainly for sport, which takes a number of forms, from trekking to racing. Horses are kept for fun and weekend recreation, but breeding establishments have been developed, and the best animals are now being sold abroad, where they command high prices.

The horses were introduced almost 1,000 years ago with the first Viking settlers. For most of this time, the stock has remained pure with no imports allowed to adulterate the strain. The animal is small, but muscular, with long, flowing mane, wide back and proud head. Unlike most horses, if it is reined in the Icelandic horse will begin to gallop, which it does remarkably well considering both its size and the toughness of the terrain. The average size of the Icelandic horse is about 13 hands. Consequently, one's feet are relatively near to the ground, which can be a problem. The sure-footed beasts pick their way through the rock-strewn countryside and it is often necessary to lift one's legs quickly out of the way of sharp rocks.

Although the Icelandic horse is one of the purest strains of any in the world, it comes in a wide range of colours. Over the centuries, only the strongest have survived the harsh weather and tough winters, and the breed today is tough, reliable, and generally amiable. It has five distinct gaits — the walk, trot and gallop, in common with other breeds, and the pace and *tölt*.These are Icelandic specialities, which allow long distances to be travelled without too much discomfort. Both are delightful to watch when the horse is being ridden by an expert. A good Icelandic horse will carry a rider day after day, as it has done for centuries.

For those interested in trekking, lack of experience is not a barrier. The horse is a perfect solution to the problem of seeing large tracts of the countryside without resorting to four-wheel drive trucks.

The idea of undertaking a long cross-country trek, spanning several days, and sleeping out or in one of the mountain huts, is a very appealing one. Riding has many advantages over walking. It is different, it allows more ground to be covered more quickly than on foot, and above all, it is fun. It is also like riding back into history because for a thousand years the horse was the only way to travel, and many of the roads and paths have been trodden by these sure-footed animals for centuries.

There is now a wide range of rides and treks to choose from, and there is something to suit all tastes. It is possible to hire a horse on the outskirts of Reykjavík and spend some time sightseeing around the edges of the city, or to sign on for a tough trek into the heartland of the country, spending many nights out.

The Icelanders take their riding seriously, and indeed, almost everyone does ride. There is no need for expensive clothes. Jeans and wellington boots are fine, together with a thick jumper, reliable waterproof and windproof jacket, and gloves. A hard hat is sensible, especially in the countryside because the ground is very rocky, but generally the animals at the trekking stables are so sure of where they are going, and so docile, that there is little fear of falling.

Equally there is very little instruction, because almost none is necessary. It takes about 3 minutes to demonstrate how to hold the reins, how to persuade the animal to turn right and left, how to stop and how to walk on.

The other marvellous thing about riding in Iceland is that it is one of the last open countries in Europe. There are no miles of barbed wire, or fences with 'keep out' notices. People respect the rules of the countryside, and the landowners allow them access to it. On a trekking trip, obviously the group stays together but individuals are actually free to go almost anywhere they want. It is a freedom that is all too rare. Iceland on horseback is an unforgettable experience.

Climbing and Skiing

There is no other area in Europe superior to Iceland for the diversity of terrain it offers to walkers, climbers and skiers. There is year-round skiing in the north, some excellent winter skiing, and of course, climbing to suit all tastes; rock climbing, full-scale mountain assaults or ice-climbing.

The interior of the country is a vast outdoor activity centre where you can learn new skills, or put old ones to the test. There are not many places where, as in Iceland, it is possible to walk day after day over glaciers and snowfields. Most of the other areas of the world offering such facilities tend to be very remote, and a visit involves major expenditure and planning.

It does not take long to fly to Iceland and one can be on the glaciers in an equally short time. Once there, a kingdom of wonder and mystery, one where several days can pass without seeing another person, is open to the visitor. Iceland is Europe's outback.

The entire centre of the country, however, does not consist of ice and snow, although it is mountainous and rugged. In the summer months, coaches travel through the heart of the mountains taking passengers to the northern coast, and there are many tracks accessible to four-wheel drive vehicles. It is even possible to cycle across Iceland, although it is necessary to carry the bicycle across the snow.

In many ways Iceland seems to be made up of many different sceneries, each stolen from a different country, but collectively like no other country on earth. In parts of the interior, the mountains and deeply carved glacial valleys are reminiscent of the Scottish Highlands, and the walking is about the same, even though the altitudes are higher. In other parts, the snow-capped peaks and glaciers are more reminiscent of the High Alps, or parts of the Himalayas.

Icelandic horses

There are many mountains to climb, and many mountain chains to ski down. It is possible to take a single day trip from Reykjavík to explore the mountains, and there are several of these climbs to choose from, such as Esja, at 909m (2,982ft), or Hengill, at 803m (2,634ft). From the top of Esja, there are the most spectacular views of Reykjavík and beyond. It is said that on a good day you can sometimes see Greenland off to the west, but it is frequently cloudy. The climb to the top is a favourite walk of the people of Reykjavík and it is said that on a summer's day, even 80-year-old women can be seen making their way to the top.

The interior of Iceland is made up of mountains and high plateaux, an uninhabited and treeless area. It rises to an average height of 500m (1,640ft) above sea level, with the highest point being in the south-east of the country.

Where the ground is not covered with glacier, there is lava sand, gravel and lava rock, which is sharp, awkwardly shaped and difficult to walk on. At this altitude, the precipitation falls as snow but all the water is drinkable, unless it is direct melt from the glacier. The rule to remember is that if the water is clear, it is safe to drink; if it is blue or

Exploration of the glaciers should only be attempted under the supervision of experienced guides

cloudy, it has come from the glacier. It can be boiled and drunk but there is usually a supply of clear water to be found.

There are maps of some of the interior, especially Skáftafell, but basic mountain crafts are needed before setting out on an expedition. The most important of these are compass reading and survival training. It is very easy for mists suddenly to swell up, or for snowstorms to take place on the very high ground. Visibility can be reduced to almost nothing and then the environment can become hostile. It is essential to be fully prepared, with full camping gear and rations at the outset of the expedition. Often the only thing to do in bad weather conditions is to pitch a tent and stay put. There are a number of mountain huts scattered about, but even for the experienced guide they are almost impossible to find in such conditions. The weather is too unpredictable and the terrain too rough to take any chances.

The best way of touring inland is to go on an arranged trip or to employ a guide. There are expeditions planned by many companies and the Iceland Travel Association also runs trips which last from a weekend to several days. Just reaching the starting point of an expedition can be an adventure. The round-the-island road system is now more than adequate, but off the beaten track, things can get a little bumpy. The Icelanders know how to drive their four-wheel vehicles, and they hurtle along seemingly unmarked trails, and splash through raging boulder-strewn rivers. More often than not, the vehicles travel in pairs, so there is usually one either to tow or push the other out of trouble. After a journey of crashing and bumping over these tracks for a few hours, it is quite a relief to get out and start walking. All the vehicles also carry two-way radios which is a reassurance.

There is a lot of skiing to be enjoyed in Iceland, mostly in the hills around the coast. Here there are increasing facilities for both alpine and cross-country skiing with ski lodges and lifts. Skiing inland is very dangerous, and best left to the most proficient. Here there are no facilities, and the terrain is generally too difficult for all but the best skiers. There is the added problem that as there are no facilities everything — tent, food, stove and so on — must be carried.

In the north, it is possible to ski in the Akureyri area all the year round, and there is the advantage of almost permanent summer daylight.

The two recommended areas for exploration and short expeditions are Kerlingarfjöll (Ogress Mountain), about 200km (125 miles) from Reykjavík, and the mountains lying behind Akureyri in the north.

The Kerlingarfjöll is a huge area in southern central Iceland and is best reached by using a rough road, Kjalvegur, which connects the north and south of the country. It is easily accessible in summer by four-wheel drive vehicles and it takes up to 8 hours to reach it from Reykjavík. On the way the route passes the Great Geysir, the glaciers of Langjökull and Hofsjökull, and close by the hot spring area of Hveravellir. The Kerlingarfjöll covers an area of almost 150sq km (58sq miles) and the mountains are cut in two by a deep gorge. The region is said to be the most varied as far as scenery and geology are concerned of any in Iceland. The mountains are reminiscent of the Alps, although they are smaller, rising (generally between 800m (2,624ft) and 1,500m (4,921ft). The mountains are particularly famous because of their striking colours, especially when the sun is shining on them. Composed mostly of tuff, basalt and liparite of varying colours, they make a marvellous subject for photography.

In the region there are also hot mud springs and steam springs where it is possible to take a bath surrounded by snow, and in places the heat has carved out strange caves and tunnels where it has broken through the snow crust.

The only road off the Kjalvegur goes to Árskard (732m, 2,400ft), which is an ideal base because there is plenty of water. It is also popular with many young Icelanders in the summer for skiing, because there is both sun and snow on the slopes of Snækollur (1,478m, 4,850ft). Courses are run here weekly for both beginners and experienced skiers. There is a hut run by the Iceland Travel Association, and in the summer it is advisable to book well in advance, because this valley is so popular.

If it is not possible to get into the hut, which is well equipped, there is camping along the rivers, where some of the most perfect pitches are to be found. The vegetation in the valley is lush, especially when compared to the starkness of the surrounding snow and ice. There are trees for shade, crystal clear water to drink, and usually a lot of warmth as the sun gets trapped in the valley.

There are many climbs within reach of the hut, and ascents of Snækollur and Árskardsfjall (919m, 3,015ft) give magnificent views into the heartland. The Hofsjökull glacier is also close but it is advisable only to venture out on to the ice with experienced guides. In places the ice is so deeply crevassed that it is necessary to walk hundreds of yards along a narrow ridge to find a point narrow enough to jump across, and then repeat the whole thing again. It is a wonderful experience, and one that should be undertaken if at all possible.

While this region is remote, the mountains around Akureyri could not be more accessible. They are easily reached by road within minutes from the town and they afford marvellous climbing, skiing and hiking. There is now a ski hotel within 10 minutes' drive from Akureyri (also within walking distance), which accommodates skiers during the late winter/early spring, and hikers during the summer. It is 500m (1,640ft) above sea level and the surrounding countryside is regarded as the best area for winter sports in Iceland. The best skiing is from mid-March to May, but the intrepid can ski all the year round by going higher.

In the summer there are a number of walks based around the ski hotel, and the staff will give you details. From here there are many interesting places to explore including the nearby Glerá Valley which is famous for its unusual flora.

The average height of the mountains around Akureyri is 1,200m

Package tours involving visits to the ice-floes are popular and can also be booked after arrival in Iceland

(4,000ft) and they are formed of basalt and some liparite. They are craggy, but climbable with care. The highest mountain in northern Iceland is Kerling, but others worth climbing are Stryta, Súlur and Kaldbakur on the other side of the fjord. The glaciers of Glerárdalsjökull and Vindheimajökull, which literally means 'Home of the Winds', can be visited. There is also some difficult rock climbing around Hraundrangar, in the Öxnadalur valley, although transport will be needed to get there. Almost anywhere in Iceland affords good climbing, but other areas recommended by the Iceland Travel Association include Snaefellsnes peninsula in the west, the Vestfirdir, Austfirdir and Myvatn.

The ITA, or the Iceland Mountaineering Club, have huts which can be used in emergencies. The areas below all have one of these huts. Thórsmörk Valley, 153km (95 miles) from Reykjavík, surrounded by glaciers and towering mountains, enjoys its own sunny micro-climate in the summer which attracts plants and birds. Landmannalaugar (185km, 115 miles, from Reykjavík), is an area famous for its hot springs, and to get there the route passes close to Hekla.

It is possible to climb Hekla because although the ascent is long, it is not too difficult. Hagavatn (149km, 92½ miles from Reykjavík) is a lake at the foot of the 'Long Glacier', called Langjökull. Hvítárnes (171km, 106 miles, from Reykjavík) is spectacular. It is another lake on the other side of the Long Glacier. The glacier actually plunges down into the water and huge chunks break away to float off as icebergs. It is possible to climb up on to the glacier behind the lake, but the waters are too cold to swim in. Rumour has it that the ITA hut here is haunted. Tindafjallajökull mountains are close to Thórsmörk but a long, hard climb is needed to reach the hut at 874m (2,867ft). On the higher slopes, up to 1,462m (4,796ft), there is permanent snow suitable for all-year-round skiing. Fimmvörduháls (180km, 112 miles from Reykjavík) is a ridge at 1,000m (3,281ft) which connects the Myrdalsjökull (1,493m, 4,898ft) and Eyjafjallajökull (1,666m, 5,466ft) glaciers. It is a good area for climbing, skiing and walking, but it is very exposed and often subject to severe weather. The Katla volcano erupted through the Myrdalsjökull in 1918.

It is essential, before spending any time out of doors in Iceland, to have the best camping and climbing gear, and it must be well proven. It can be very windy on the exposed slopes and extra guys will be needed for tents. The ground is extremely hard and special tent pegs will be needed. Lightweight, cheap pegs will simply buckle and be useless. It can get very cold on the mountains so a three-season bag is necessary, or even a four-season bag if you are out in early spring. A reliable tent is a must, and one that has proved it can stand up to gale force winds and heavy falls of snow. For the sake of a little extra weight, a survival bag, especially a Gore-Tex type, is a good idea.

Climbers will need crampons, snow axe and ropes; these are advisable even if you are just crossing snow or glaciers. Other essential pieces of equipment are a whistle, and a first aid kit. Clothing must be warm, windproof and waterproof. Temperature fluctuations can be enormous between the hot sun in the valleys, and the bitterly cold winds on an exposed snow face. Thick trousers or breeches are advisable, together with warm shirt, jumper and ano-rak. Waterproof jacket and overtrousers are necessary, and gaiters are useful to keep out the wet snow and small stones. A warm hat and gloves will help keep in the heat, and a pair of sturdy shoes, mountain boots or 'bog trotters' completes the kit.

Many Icelanders wear wellington boots because they are ideal for wading across the many streams. If the water is too deep, it is also quite easy to remove these boots and wade over. There are now quite a lot of combination boots available, mostly of Scandinavian origin, which combine the sole of a mountain boot with the upper of a wellington. This gives greater waterproofing together with grip. Do not just wade across and hope your boots will dry out. It is a recipe for blisters or worse as the water can be very cold and boots just do not dry. Take boots and socks off and stow them in your rucksack. Some people carry a spare pair of socks to slip on when fording a stream so that they do not slip on the submerged rocks. Obviously, if you are out on the trail for some days, a spare set of clothing is essential as well as food and fuel.

Iceland is a country that has a great deal to offer outdoor enthusiasts, and the rules to follow are the rules any sensible climber or walker would stick to. Be prepared; do not attempt to do too much; let someone know where you are going and how long you expect to be away; and do not be afraid to ask for advice. The Iceland Travel Association, Iceland Mountaineering Club or various travel companies are only too willing to help you.

Walking and Hiking

Almost everything that has been said about climbing in Iceland can be applied to walking and hiking, except that there is much more room to do it in; the central highlands, the mountains and glaciers, along the fjords on the east and west coasts; the beautiful countryside around Lake Myvatn are all ideal walking areas.

The major difference between walking or backpacking in Iceland as opposed to the Scottish Highlands, or the Alps, is simply the remoteness of the place. It is quite possible to be several days away from the nearest farm so there are problems with logistics. Everything must be carried, and it is necessary to be self-reliant and competent. It is a daunting thought that the nearest telephone might be 2 or 3 days' hard walking away.

The remoteness of Iceland and its northerly position also means that the weather can be much more inhospitable than that of countries further south. It is quite possible that in the mountains the weather can turn nasty; it can quickly close in, or snow, and ferocious Atlantic gales frequently come rushing in. It is this very remoteness, however, which forms a great part of Iceland's attraction.

In planning any expedition into the mountains on foot, it is necessary to discover first what current conditions are like from either the Iceland Travel Association, Iceland Mountaineering Club, local hotel or even local farmer. Always err on the side of caution when packing, and take more than necessary rather than less. Have enough spare clothes, extra rations, and fuel to last, and an adequate supply of waterproof matches. There are not many trees in Iceland and it is a crime to chop them down for firewood, so fuel must be carried to heat food or water. There are suppliers of gas cylinders in all main centres, and most garages also stock them. It is also possible to get paraffin at a number of garages and obviously petroleum.

In many places you will have to camp on rock or very hard ground, so take suitable tent pegs — ones that will not buckle as they are being banged into the ground, and which can be retrieved when packing up. The weather can turn very quickly and gales can rush in from the sea, so extra guys are a good idea. The wind can also play havoc with attempts to cook. Unless you can get good shelter you will not get maximum use from your fuel if the wind is constantly blowing the flames about. A ridge tent or dome with an awning or extension is ideal for both storage and cooking.

If driving and camping weight is no problem, you can keep a lot of food in the vehicle. If you are backpacking you must always have emergency supplies to cover you for a couple of days, and stock up whenever you have the opportunity. There is a 10kg (22lb) limit on imported food (and some products are banned), but as food is expensive, it is sensible to bring in the staple and dearest items. Things like milk, cheese and bread are readily available and the bread lasts for days very well.

Most people prefer to use their own tried and tested equipment, but if you want to cut your weight down while travelling to and from Iceland, there are a number of camping suppliers.

It may be easier to participate in an organised walking holiday. In these, before the group arrives, advance food depots have been set up which not only means less to carry but also a more varied diet along the way. Groups must still be fit, however, and loads of 20kg (44lb) are normal.

The weather still catches many people unawares, especially the glare of the summer sun reflected off snow. Sunglasses are advisable as well as suntan cream and lip salve. In various parts of the country, especially around Lake Myvatn in August and early September, mosquito repellent is a good idea.

It is a good idea too to join the Youth Hostel Association and carry an International Card, if you are planning a walking holiday in Iceland. There are youth hostels to stay in, or mountain huts to make a change from canvas, and such a night indoors can be a welcome relief.

Camping is permitted almost anywhere except in national parks and nature reserves; even here special areas are usually provided for campers and these are normally signposted. It is polite to ask a farmer for permission to camp on his land if you are near the farmhouse, or near fenced land. There are maps of the interior but they tend to be rather lacking in detail and too much reliance should not be placed on them. Efforts are now being made to produce accurate large scale maps of the most popular areas, and there are good map shops in all the towns. Being able to read a map is an important asset, and everyone should be able to use a compass. Often when the clouds close in, and visibility is nil, it is still possible to continue using the compass bearing. Remember, however, that compass variations will be greater in Iceland then countries further south. Almost every community has a campsite nearby, usually with toilet and water laid on, but not always. The campsites near large communities can usually be recognised by the toilet which is housed in a tall, steep-sided wooden hut, all roof and no walls. Some campsites are free, but a small charge is made at others and it is wise to enquire just in case.

Iceland is a magnificent country to explore. It is a harsh, rugged countryside which is at times daunting, but almost always magnificent. There can be few finer holidays than a week or two in Iceland with a rucksack and the freedom to go where you please. The only other essential item is a camera, and plenty of film. It is advisable to take as much film as you will require into Iceland with you because it is very expensive to buy locally.

2
REYKJAVÍK AND THE
SOUTH-WEST

T he first introduction to Iceland is **Keflavík**, important as the site of the international airport, as a trading centre, and for its closeness to the United States air base, which is part of NATO's North Atlantic command. In fact, until the new airport terminal was opened, one's first impression of the island was misleading, with American-style cinemas, social clubs and American spellings until the route to Reykjavík headed out into the typical Icelandic land-scape. The thermal activity around Keflavík is evident as clouds of smoke and steam burst from fissures in the ground, and the smell of sulphur can be strong in the air.

Keflavík has been an important trading centre for at least 500 years. There are records that German traders landed on the coast here as early as 1500.

Originally Keflavík was a series of farms owned by the Bishop of Skálholt and the name is recorded as far back as 1300. These church estates eventually passed to the Danish Crown. An early English record of 1540 reports that a merchant from Ipswich in England traded there from 1513, and the presence of the German traders is reflected in some of the Germanic names in the area. Keflavík received its first official trading licence in 1566 which was awarded to a German merchant from Hamburg called Jochim Thim, but trading powers reverted to Danish merchants after the Monopoly was introduced by the Danish king in 1602.

Keflavík achieved town status in 1949 and is currently enjoying a boom. It has become the second largest export port in Iceland, there is a flourishing fishing industry and many other industries. It has a population of well over 6,000 and there is an enormous amount of building going on, as there is in all the towns and villages in the south-west peninsula.

Keflavík has a hospital, a swimming pool, a sports ground, three hotels, cinema and many garages, shops and restaurants and an indoor sports hall. There is an interesting craft museum, the Vatnsnes, which shows the tools and equipment used by tradesmen and craftsmen of the area in the past.

For the 50km (30 mile) drive into Reykjavík, the road follows the southern shore of Hafnarfjördur along the northern shore of the Reykjanes peninsula. This stretch of road is dual carriageway, a luxury in Iceland. On the landward side there is a huge grey gravelly lava desert, with huge piles of clinker-type rocks thrown up into strange shapes. Occasionally, there are mosses and lichens, but this is a treeless landscape looking very much like the aftermath of some massive open mining project. The landscape, however, shows just how new the country is, the rocks lie piled as they were heaved up from the ground, and the vegetation still has not had time to take a hold, although it becomes lusher as one nears Reykjavík.

One has still to remember that this is still an earthquake area — a continuation of the mid-Atlantic fault — and many of the lava domes and craters have huge cracks and fissures. There are a few scattered houses along the shores of the fjord, and it is a barren landscape inland — green and brown mosses and lichens and black lava. Occasionally there are patches of tufted rough grass, and for a few brief weeks, the scenery is brightened by clusters of wild purple lupins.

You can also spot some way from the road, wooden trellises which are used to dry the fish. Huge quantities of cod heads are still exported to Africa, and these can be spotted suspended from the wooden frames.

It is perhaps worth stopping off at the **Blue Lagoon**, just off the road from Keflavík to Reykjavík. There is no mistaking it, because on the other side of the natural lake, there is a power plant which harnesses all the free heat. A small hotel has now been built by the

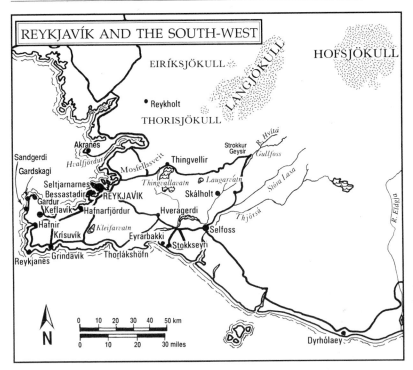

REYKJAVÍK AND THE SOUTH-WEST

EIRÍKSJÖKULL

Reykholt

THORISJÖKULL

LANGJÖKULL

HOFSJÖKULL

Akranes

Sandgerdi
Gardskagi
Hvalfjördur
Mosfellssveit

Seltjarnarnes
Bessastadir
Gardur
Keflavík
Hafnarfjördur
Hafnir
Krísuvík
Reykjanes
Grindavík
Thorlákshöfn

REYKJAVÍK

Thingvellir
Thingvallavatn
Skálholt

Strokkur
Geysir
Gullfoss
R. Hvítá
Laugarvatn
Stóra Laxa

Hveragerdi
Thjórsá

Kleifarvatn
Eyrárbakki
Stokkseyri
Selfoss

Dyrhólaey

R. Eldgjá

N

0 10 20 30 40 50 km

0 10 20 30 miles

lagoon and there is a pathway down to the water. The water is a strange, almost cloudy blue, thick with all the chemicals coming up from below the ground with the rising water. It is not a good place to swim if you have open cuts, although the waters are said to be very beneficial for people with skin diseases. You can have a dip at the pool, and then take a shower before continuing your journey, or you could book into the hotel for a night to give you more time to explore this fascinating geological area.

The popularity of the Blue Lagoon is increasing and a growing number of people suffering from skin problems now fly to Iceland for treatment there. Facilities for the bathers, with changing rooms and showers, are constantly being improved, and a little sandy beach has now been created on the hotel side of the lagoon.

If you continue along Route 41 towards Reykjavík you can spot away to the right, one of the most recognisable features in southern

The Blue Lagoon

Iceland, the cone of **Keilir**, which rises to almost 380m (1,246ft) beyond the stark lavafield of Strandarheidi.

Ahead and in the distance, are the huge red and white striped towers of the Straumsvík aluminium works, and beyond the first glimpses of Reykjavík across the water. The landscape starts to improve, there is more greenery, and horses, cattle and sheep graze. The road then skirts the fast growing town and port of Hafnarfjördur. You can turn off left here to visit Álftanes, the peninsula which houses the president's official residence at Bessastadir. Just before Hafnarfjördur, you can turn right on Route 42 which takes you south through the lava deserts and mountains into a very active geothermal area.

You can get out of your vehicle at Krísuvík, and walk around the jets of steam gushing from the ground, and the scalding hot, bubbling mud pools. There are signs warning you that the area is dangerous, and you must keep to the path. It is an exciting introduction to a country that is still shaping itself under your feet.

One of the first things you have to learn when travelling around in Iceland is that the atmosphere is so unpolluted, and the sunlight so intense, that even in bad weather, things always look much closer than they really are. It is quite possible to see 40 or 50km (25 or 30 miles) in good visibility, so when you start to see the multi-coloured roofs of Reykjavík, it still is a fair distance away.

There has been a tremendous amount of building going on in the south-west, and all the major settlements around Reykjavík are expanding fast.

Reykjavík, the smokeless city, is the most northerly capital in the world, lying north of the 64th parallel. It was the home of Iceland's first settler; when Ingólfur Arnarson landed on the southern shores of Faxa Bay in south-west Iceland in 874 he made his way inland until he found a large lake and it was by this that he built his homestead. According to the Sagas when Ingólfur Arnarson first sighted land, he threw the religious 'pillars' overboard and swore that he would settle where they came ashore. Thus he came to the lake named Tjörnin (which literally means 'The Pond'). He must have been impressed by the geysers and hot steam pouring from the ground, and maybe it was because of this that he called the place Reykjavík, which means 'Smoky Bay'. Like many other things, the name conjures up a completely false impression. Iceland is not a land of ice, and Reykjavík is not smoky. In fact, because all heating and hot water is supplied naturally from deep in the ground, there is no need to burn fossil fuels, so Reykjavík is one of the most smoke-free cities in the world. The lake near which he settled is still in the centre of the city which now houses a third of the island's population.

The first sight of Reykjavík comes when approached from the international airport at Keflavík 30 miles away. Suddenly in the distance, across the bay, the multi-coloured roofs of Reykjavík can be seen. Corrugated iron is still the favourite roofing material in the town and residents paint them a host of colours which adds to the capital's charm.

Reykjavík is the heart of the country because within its boundaries and the surrounding towns, more than half the population of the country is to be found. The census in 1860 showed Reykavík had a population of around 700, against a total island population of just under 50,000. The city's population had risen to more than 11,500 by 1910 and now stands at 87,000 out of the country's total population of 250,000. The city houses the commercial, governmental and cultural life of the country and contains all the official government ministries, as well as the libraries and museums recording the country's heritage.

Reykjavík is a modern capital with skyscrapers, international standard hotels and restaurants, but it also has a remarkable old world charm and there are many old buildings which add to this character. It is a city full of contrast, from the bustling harbour and fishing port with its evocative smells and excellent fish restaurants, to the bustle of the modern shopping centre a short walk away.

The old centre has been carefully preserved, and many old buildings have been uprooted and rebuilt in the Folk Museum, in Arbaer, one of the eastern suburbs. There is a surprising number of trees in Reykjavík, as well as ponds and lakes teeming with tame birdlife, many of the species considered rare in the British Isles, and gardens with neatly cut lawns and borders of brilliantly coloured flowers. The city sprawls leisurely around the bay, and despite the fact that it is the country's capital, there is an air of relaxation. The people of Reykjavík work hard and play hard. Many will visit one of the open-air swimming pools before breakfast, and it is not unusual to see elderly men and women in their 70s and 80s walking around the pool in their swimming costumes even though the air temperature is only a few degrees above freezing. Many office workers go for a swim before going in to work and housewives will often call in to do

Brightly painted properties in Lækjargata, Reykjavík

Hateigskirkja Reykjavík

Reykjavík's main outdoor swimming pool

a few lengths before going home to make breakfast for their families.

There are many lovely old buildings to see in Reykjavík including the Parliament House, built in 1881, and the old Government Building which dates from the middle of the eighteenth century. Both are in the old centre of Reykjavík between the harbour and the lake. Nearby are the National Library and the National Theatre which are next to each other and close to the statue of Ingólfur Arnarson. Other sites worth visiting are the University, National Museum and Nordic House, which was designed by the world famous Finnish architect Alvar Aalto. There are many churches, including the old cathedral near to the Parliament House, and the towering new Hallgrímskirkja, the city's most recently built church.

The traditional buildings of Reykjavík are to be found in the Folk Museum at Árbaer. The open-air collection houses several old buildings as well as a fine old church and farmhouse, both turf-roofed, which date back to the beginning of this century.

Most of the older houses are built with wood, but cement is now being used widely in construction, especially for the large estates of flats which are now springing up. Iceland has a policy of promoting

PLACES OF INTEREST IN REYKJAVÍK

The oldest part of the city is between the Tjörnin Lake and the harbour and includes two squares, Austurvóllur and Laekjartorg. Further east, away from the sea can be found the newer shopping areas, cinemas and theatres but everywhere can be reached on foot without any difficulty.

Adalstraeti 10

The city's oldest building dating back to 1752, 34 years before Reykjavík was granted city status. It was built originally as a storage shed. Another of the oldest surviving houses is **Stjórnarrádid**, in Laekjargata, built in the eighteenth century as a jail. It is now Government House, accommodating the offices of the president and prime minister.

Árbær Folk Museum

An open-air museum on the city outskirts in which one can find old buildings brought mainly from Reykjavík, including an interesting turf-roofed wooden and stone church from the nearby town of Hafnarfjördur.

Arnarhóll

Literally Eagle's Mound, is near Laekjartorg and has an imposing statue of Ingólfur Arnarson looking out to sea.

The Árni Magnusson Institute, at Arnagardur
The Manuscript Institute

Part of the University, housing the ancient Icelandic manuscripts now returned from Copenhagen.

Ásgrímur Jónsson Gallery

An exhibition of paintings by one of Iceland's most famous artists in his house which he left to the nation.

Ásmundur Sveinsson Sculptures

Many of Sveinsson's sculptures can be seen in the parks of Reykjavík but most of his works, including his recent metal mobiles, are to be found in the garden and private gallery at his dome-shaped home in the city. It is sometimes possible to visit the sculptor's studio. For more information contact the Tourist Office.

Austurvóllur

A square in the centre of the city with a statue of Jón Sigurdsson (1811-79), one of the leaders in the island's fight for national independence. The square is on the site of Ingólfur Arnarson's original farmstead.

Botanical Garden

Garden and small park near the outdoor sports stadium.

Catholic Cathedral

The only Catholic church in Iceland.

Einar Jónsson Museum

Houses a collection of sculptures with an Icelandic influence. Close by is the statue of Leif Eiríksson, the Viking who discovered America 500 years before

Columbus. The statue was a gift to the people of Iceland from the Government of the United States and it stands outside the new Lutheran cathedral, Hallgrímskirkja.

Fálkahúsid
The Falcon House, home of the Iceland Handicrafts Centre in Hafnarstraeti. It used to be where Icelandic falcons, the gyrfalcon, were kept before being sent to the court of the King of Denmark. Today the roof bears two impressive carvings of falcons, on either side of a Viking ship.

Hallgrímskirkja
Twentieth-century church, lift to steeple.

Kjarvalsstadir
Art gallery in the Miklatún Park.

Lutheran Cathedral
Eighteenth-century, much renovated.

Maritime Museum
An exhibition of boatbuilding up to the twentieth century.

Menntaskólinn
Now a high school, overlooking Laekjargata, used to be the meeting place for the Althing before the present parliament building was opened. It dates back to 1846.

National Museum and Art Gallery
Featuring Icelandic history and culture.

Natural History Museum
Small but interesting collection, including a specimen of the extinct great auk bird.

Nordic Centre
Has a library and exhibition devoted to the Nordic way of life. It also stages concerts and film shows.

Numismatic Collection
Display of coins, decorations and books.

Parliament House
The Althing, seat of the oldest legislative body in the world, founded in AD930.

Post and Telecommunications History Museum
A new museum covering the history of telecommunications on the island.

Sundlaug Vesturbæjar
An open-air swimming pool. A modern building and popular pool heated by water from the natural hot springs, with facilities for sunbathing.

Sundlaugar Reykjavíkur
Swimming stadium where international swimming contests are sometimes staged. Both Sundlaug Vesturbæjar and Sundlaugar Reykjavíkur offer excellent sauna facilities.

The Volcano Show
Hellusund
A 2-hr-long award-winning programme of films about volcanoes and nature. The films are screened nightly during the summer at 8pm in English, except on Sundays and Mondays.

Reykjavík's harbour (above) and Lake Tjörnin (below)

Hotel Borg in Posthstræti, Reykjavík

house-ownership, and very cheap loans are made available for families wishing to own their own property.

The best way to see Reykjavík is still on foot, although taxis and a regular bus service are available for the less mobile, or those wishing to go further afield. Taxis are plentiful and cheap and can be hailed in the street or ordered by telephone. All the top hotels have direct lines to the taxi companies. The cabs can be identified either because they have the word 'taxi' displayed, or they have a sign bearing the letter 'L' on a yellow background.

The main bus station is at Hlemmur, at the junction of Laugavegur, Hverfisgata and Raudarárstígur. There are frequent services both in and around the city. If you plan to spend some time in Reykjavík, it is a good idea to buy tickets in advance because it is cheaper. Bus stops are marked with the letters 'SVR'. There is only one fare on all routes, and the drivers are not allowed to give change. Discount tickets are available from the drivers and at Laekjargata, Hlemmur, Grensás and Borgartún 35. If you need more than one bus to get to your destination, ask the driver for a transfer ticket (*skiptimidi* in Icelandic and pronounced *skiptimithi*) when entering the first bus.

Parking in the centre of Reykjavík, as with any large city, can be a problem although there are car parks and parking meters. It is best to park on the outskirts, or leave your car in the hotel car park, and either walk or use public transport.

The harbour, where fishing boats are unloaded, can be visited, followed by the National Museum or the Árni Magnusson Institute, which houses the priceless Saga manuscripts. A visit to the hot water storage tanks above the city gives remarkable views across Reykjavík and the bay beyond, with the towering Mount Esja in the background. There is no better sight than to watch the fishing boats return late in the evening with the midnight sun lighting the sky.

Shops in the main shopping area are open Monday to Friday from 9am-6pm, and from 10am-4pm on Saturdays. Some supermarkets stay open later on Thursdays and Fridays. Many shops, however, close on Saturdays during June, July and August. There are also two public holidays during the summer — National Day on 17 June, and Bankers Holiday on 1 August.

Post offices are usually open from 8.30/9am to 4.30/5pm, although the branch in the BSI bus terminal is open to 7.30pm on weekdays and between 8am and 3pm on Saturdays. Banking hours are 9.15am to 4pm Monday to Friday, although most hotels can exchange currency. The main shopping areas are Adalstraeti, Austurstraeti, Hverfisgata, Bankastraeti, Laugavegur and Skólavördustígur. Public toilets are not common in Reykjavík but they are available at Bankastraeti, about forty yards or so from Laekjartorg Square, at Hlemmur bus station, in the pedestrian tunnel under Miklabraut at Langahlíd, on the south-east corner of Miklatún, and in the Hljómskálagardur park, just to the south of Tjörnin.

A new tourist information centre has been opened at Ingólfsstraeti 5. It is open from 8.30am to 7pm Monday to Fridays, from 8.30am to 4pm on Saturdays, and 10am to 12noon on Sundays during the summer. It has a large collection of videos about the island and its mini-cinema where you can view them. There is also an English language monthly newspaper, *News from Iceland* which gives details of news and events, and you can even take out a subscription to have it delivered when you get home.

When driving or travelling around the country, look out for the *'i'* for information sign, where you can get advice on local sights, campsites, accommodation and so on.

There are two professional theatres, an opera house, ten cinemas and a biennial art festival. There is also a film festival, and several fine galleries. For nature lovers there are many fine walks in and around the city which enable you to see the country's rich birdlife at close hand. Another source of surprise to visitors is that one of the best salmon rivers in Iceland runs through the centre of the city.

There are more than eighty fine restaurants in Reykjavík serving many of the country's speciality dishes. Some of the best fish in the world can be tried at the restaurants around the harbour.

The cuisine of Iceland tends to be international, especially in the bigger hotels but there are many local dishes which should be tried. The local salmon and trout are, of course, magnificent and can be served in a variety of ways. Herring, too, come in many preserves and flavours. Then there are shrimps and small lobsters which are caught off the south coast. You must try *graflax*, raw salmon pressed with special herbs, and quite delicious, and Iceland's cheap caviare.

It is not surprising that lamb and mutton figure largely in the diet because there are so many sheep on the island. One traditional dish is smoked mutton called *hangikjöt*, and another, *svid*, calls for a tougher constitution. It is a whole sheep's head which has been boiled, and it is usually presented complete on a plate. Although not a pretty sight, and quite a challenge to eat, it is worth the effort.

Ptarmigan, the island's most prolific game bird, is served in a rich sauce, and the dish is called *rjúpa*. *Thorramatur* on the menu usually means pickled meats, while dried fish is served as *hardfiskur*. Also worth trying, especially for breakfast is *skyr*, a sour yoghurt that is eaten with sugar and cream.

Two other specialities are raw shark, known as *hákarl*, and *hverabraud*, a ryebread baked in the ground in the heat of the thermal soil. There are many stories about how *hákarl* is prepared, and most are enough to put you off the dish, but it is a delicacy worth trying. Because the country lies in the path of the Gulf Stream many sharks can be found off the coast. When one is caught and killed, it is buried in the ground and the position marked. After a certain length of time, the fish is dug up and strips of the raw flesh eaten. It has a most unpleasant smell but does taste delicious, even though to some this may be an acquired taste.

Most restaurants and hotels will serve wine with the meal, and cocktails and spirits before and after. Strong beer is now available, although low alcohol or alcohol-free beer is more widely on sale. The island's home brew is a fiery spirit known as *brennivín*, which is also

Information booth in the Austurstræti, Reykjavík

Thingvellir

affectionately called Black Death. A measure of *brennivín* in the beer can be a wonderful pick-me-up, while two or three are likely to knock you down. Hotels and restaurants in the capital normally serve alcohol from noon to 2.30pm and from 7pm to closing time which is around midnight. The cocktail bars of the bigger hotels will stay open later. There are no bars in Iceland and when you see a 'bar' sign it normally means a snack bar where you can get light refreshments, coffee or non-alcoholic drinks. Pubs are becoming more popular, the first one opening in 1985. They are more like wine bars, but you can get food as well as beer, wine and spirits. They are good places to meet and many have live music. Most have dress codes and employ doormen to enforce them.

Leaving Reykjavík, other places of interest to visit in the south-west area of Iceland include **Bessastadir**, in Álftanes; this is the official residence of the President of Iceland. It once belonged to Snorri Sturluson, but the estate later became the property of the Crown and the residence of the Danish Governor. For a time it was the seat of higher education in the country but has been the presidential residence since Iceland became a republic in 1944. The magnificent white buildings are among the oldest in Iceland, some dating back to 1763, and the fine old church, also painted white, is well worth a visit.

Heidmörk, to the east of the capital, is a public park that actually belongs to Reykjavík. Although the capital has many trees and bushes, they are not so common outside urban areas, and the park is a popular place for people seeking a little peace. The grounds contain a large number of different species of bushes.

Krísuvík is 36km (21 miles) south of Reykjavík, and it is an interesting area of hot springs. A long time ago there used to be a sulphur mine there. It is now surrounded by lavafields which give the impression of a very lunar landscape.

Hvalfjördur, to the north of the capital, is the longest fjord in the south-west. It is very deep, and served as a naval base for the Allies during World War II, although the base has now been demolished. Iceland's only whaling station is situated in Hvalfjördur and the landing and cutting of whales has been a great attraction during the summer, with coachloads of visitors arriving from Reykjavík. The future of the station is now in doubt because Iceland, as a party to the international whaling agreement, has decided to stop whaling. The whaling station may be converted so that it can be used for other forms of fish processing, or it may be left as it is, as a museum to an industry which is fast disappearing.

Akranes is one of the largest fishing ports in the country and also has the only cement factory in Iceland. There is a daily ferry boat connection with Reykjavík, and the town has hotels, guest houses, restaurants and a camping site at Gardabraut. There is a tourist information centre, hospital, swimming pool, indoor sports stadium, a cinema and a folk museum. There is also a fine sandy beach and a golf course.

Thingvellir, 50km (31 miles) to the east of Reykjavík, is the national shrine of Iceland and one of its most beautiful places. The oldest existing parliament in the world first met here in AD930. It has always been the focal point for the country, and whenever a major event is to be celebrated, thousands of people come here. At the celebration of the 1,100th anniversary of the first settlement on Iceland in 1974, more than 60,000 people packed into Thingvellir.

Nearby Lögberg is the cliff overlooking the place where the Althing (assembly) met, and speakers stood to address the gatherings from this point. Nearby is Drekkingarhylur, the drowning pool, where mothers of illegitimate children were drowned. It is sited in the river in Almannagjá, a lava gorge, which with the Oxarárfoss waterfall, is an impressive sight.

Peningagjá is the Money Chasm, and people still throw coins into the clear waters. The coins give off strange reflections as they drop through the water, but it is said that if you can follow your coin all the way down until it comes to rest on the bottom, your wish will come true.

There is an old church at Thingvellir, and the pastor is also warden of the national park, which covers part of the area. Beside the church is the national burial ground.

Thingvallavatn is the largest lake in Iceland 83sq km (32sq miles) and 100m (328ft) deep, and nearby is Valhöll, a hotel and excellent restaurant that is open for the summer months only.

A few miles to the east of Thingvellir is Laugarvatn, an education centre beside a lovely lake of the same name. During the summer months, the schools become hotels and the area is a popular tourist resort. One of the main attractions is the natural hot water saunas. There is a small changing room, where for a few pence you can strip and shower before walking to the wooden sauna cubicles. There are very strict hygiene standards in Iceland and it is compulsory to shower before entering any swimming pool or sauna.The saunas stand side by side; one is hot and the other very hot. The most hardy prefer to have a sauna and then plunge into the very cold lake. However, it is as well to note that the saunas can be quite overpowering, if you are not used to them, be careful at first.

Gullfoss, east of Laugarvatn, is the best-known waterfall in Iceland, and it is spectacular on a sunny day. It is 32m (100ft) high and the spray splashes up into the sky so that if the sun is shining, it produces a beautiful rainbow. Perhaps the only problem with Gullfoss is photographing. There is a small monument at the fall to Iceland's first conservationist, Sigrídur Tómasdóttir, a farmer's wife who successfully resisted attempts to have the watercourse altered. She looks out today at the falls she saved.

Geysir, 30km (18½ miles) south-east of Laugarvatn, gave the world the word geyser. It can send up columns of water 60m (200ft) high. For many years it was inactive, but as previously mentioned, the warden of the area has found a way of persuading it to come to life, by throwing bars of carbolic soap into the bubbling crater. It is an incredible sight. Gradually, as more soap is thrown in, the water in the

Gullfoss in summer and winter

mouth of the crater begins to bubble more vigorously, and a great deal of foam is created. The bubbles get bigger and bigger until they form spouts into the air, and then suddenly with a roaring rush, the geyser flings its water column upwards.

Close by is **Strokkur**, a much smaller but very active geyser, which constantly bubbles and spouts. A great achievement with Strokkur is to photograph it just before it spouts. The crater gradually fills with water until it is level with the top. Then the pressure from below forces the surface water upwards forming a bubble, and the trick is to photograph it just before the bubble bursts and the water is sent shooting upwards. There is a small hostel near the geysers, as well as a garage and snack bar.

A good way of seeing all these sights, if you do not have your own transport, is to take a bus from Reykjavík. There are daily round trips, both guided and unguided, from the capital taking in both Gullfoss and Geysir; some trips visit Thingvellir as well.

Skálholt, to the south-east of Laugarvatn, is steeped in history. It was the greatest centre for learning in Old Iceland, and was the episcopal seat for southern Iceland from 1056 to 1796. All that remains of these times, however, is a tunnel that ran from the old church and farm to the school. There is now a new church on the site.

Back at the coast, **Seltjarnarnes** lies alongside Reykjavík and attained municipal status in 1974. There is some industry (mostly fishing), but it is really a dormitory town for the capital. There is a large sports hall, swimming pool and community centre.

Mosfellssveit has developed a great deal in the last few years, as residents of Reykjavík have moved out to build larger houses and apartments. Again, it is mostly a dormitory town supplying the capital with workers, although there is some industry, notably the Álafoss factories which produce woollen goods.

Kópavogur has grown faster than any other town in Iceland. There were few buildings before the last war, but today there are buildings everywhere and it is a thriving community. A new civic centre is being built and there are cinemas, swimming pool and a disco.

Between Kópavogur and Hafnarfjördur is **Gardabaer**, most of whose residents work in the capital. The town does have a shipbuilding yard, as well as metal and chemical industries. The landscape of Gardabaer is very varied, and the old lava that once flowed from Búrfell to the sea has taken on strange forms.

Hafnarfjördur, a fishing port, is the home port of many trawlers. The fishing industry is the basis of its inhabitants' employment, although a number of other industries have sprung up. The town is located on a fjord which provides an excellent natural harbour. The volcano Búrfell, about 5km (3 miles) east of the fjord, erupted 7,000 years ago. The lava flowed along the northern side of the fjord forming a high, sheltering wall, creating a natural harbour.

At the beginning of the fifteenth century, the English started to trade with Icelanders. Hafnarfjördur became an English trading port and remained so for about three-quarters of a century, as it had one of the best harbours in the south-west part of Iceland, and there were rich fishing banks just off the coast. German merchants then started to compete with the English for special rights and facilities in Hafnarfjördur, and there are accounts of a battle between the two groups in the town, which ended with a German victory. After this, the Germans were virtually in full control of Hafnarfjördur. They built houses, commercial buildings and a church.

At the beginning of the seventeenth century the Danish king issued a decree to the effect that only Danish subjects with special trade licences could trade with Iceland. The Danish trade monopoly was in force until the year 1787 — almost two centuries. Some enterprises founded then still existed in the town when it was given municipal rights in the year 1908, although by then, most had passed into the ownership of Icelanders.

Near Hafnarfjördur and towards the hot springs area in Krísuvík, there are three lavafields created by separate eruptions. First is the Hvaleyrar lavafield, whose exact age has not yet been determined. Next is a younger field of lava which flowed about 2,200 years ago, cooling off and solidifying before it managed to reach the sea, called Óbrynnishólabruni. Then a low mountain range called Undirhlídar comes into view. The road goes through a pass in the range, called Vatnaskard. On the hillsides are extinct craters from a volcanic eruption in the period following the settlement of the country, and the new lava flowed from there over the older lavafield, Óbrynnishóla-bruni, and all the way into the sea at Straumsvík on the coast south of Hafnarfjördur. There the lava-flow formed a wall, creating a sheltered natural harbour, in much the same way as the harbour at Hafnarfjördur was formed. This lavafield is called Kapelluhraun and derives its name from a chapel built there in Catholic times in honour of St Barbara.

Monument to Sigrídur Tómasdóttir, Gullfoss

Strokkur

PLACES OF INTEREST IN THE SOUTH-WEST

Eyrarbakki
Fishing town containing Danish merchant's house, one of the oldest buildings in Iceland, dating from 1765. Notable beach.

Gullfoss (The Golden Waterfall)
One of the most impressive waterfalls in Europe. On a sunny day a rainbow forms over the falls, adding to the spectacle of the foaming glacier river Hvítá tumbling into the deep gorge below.

Haukadalur
A geyser field only a few miles from Gullfoss. The **Great Geysir**, which gave its name to hot springs all over the world, seems to be almost dormant at present and only rarely spouts — but the nearby **Strokkur Geyser** sends a fountain of hot water and steam high into the sky every few minutes.

Hveragerdi
This is an area of hot springs — and a visit to Hveragerdi shows you how cleverly the Icelanders have made use of this important natural fuel resource. Glasshouses in the valley are heated by steam from the hot springs, enabling such exotic fruits as bananas and grapes, as well as salad ingredients, to be grown. Iceland is almost self-sufficient in horticultural produce.

Past Vatnaskard is the Lake Kleifarvatn. Brooks from the surrounding hills empty into it, but no outlet is visible.

Close to Hafnarfjördur is the aluminium factory in **Straumsvík**, which is Swiss-owned and which imports its raw materials from Australia. The huge red and white striped towers of the plant can be seen from Reykjavík quite clearly on good days. There is also a factory producing electrical appliances, the only one of its kind in Iceland. At the turn of the century, the town only had a population of about 374 but now it is well over 12,000.

Vogar is a small fishing town which, with surrounding **Vatnsley-suströnd**, has a population of just a few hundred.

Njardvík, is another town whose roots are firmly in the fishing industry. It has a good harbour and many fishing-related industries, as does **Gardur**, which also boasts one of the island's best golf courses. At **Gardskagi**, at the northern tip of the peninsula, there is

Krísuvík
This is another area of hot springs, approached through an extensive moon-like landscape of contorted lava. The route passes through the pretty little town of Hafnarfjördur, and the excursion may be conveniently arranged to include a visit to the church and president's residence at Bessastadir on the Álftanes peninsula between Hafnarfjördur and Reykjavík.

Lake Hredavatn
A popular summer resort located in the fertile Borgarfjördur district.

Lake Laugarvatn
A good centre for country excursions and pony-trekking to such places as Thingvellir, Gullfoss and Geysir. Good hotel accommodation, hot springs, a sauna bath and a swimming pool.

Stokkseyri
Contains Rjómabúid — an interesting folk museum.

Thingvellir
Not only is Thingvellir in an impressive location on Lake Thingvallavatn, but it is also the most historic site in the island. Here the Althing met once a year to make laws, including the law passed in AD1000 to introduce Christianity into Iceland. A big part of Thingvellir is now a National Park.

Thjórsárdalur Valley
Containing at Stöng the excavated ruins of a farm dating from the twelfth century, and the nearby Búrfell hydro-electric power station with good views of Mount Hekla.

a very varied birdlife, so it is a good place for ornithologists, while nearby **Sandgerdi** is another small fishing village with a population of just over 1,000.

Hafnir is a small village standing on the banks of Ósbotnar, a small bay. It is especially well worth visiting, because it can trace its roots back for centuries.

Grindavík, on the southern coast of the Reykjanes peninsula, is a bustling fishing port, and fishing accounts for most of its livelihood. There is a community centre, health care centre, and, of course, a swimming pool.

It now has more than 2,000 inhabitants and was granted municipal rights in 1974. The town is a good base to explore the area and coastline, with its rich birdlife, and the Reykjanes National Park. There is a campsite and guesthouse, and a café near the harbour where you can mingle with the fishermen. Nearby is a statue called

Hope, which shows a fisherman's family looking out to sea awaiting his homecoming.

Thorlákshöfn is a town whose population used to swell dramatically during the fishing season. For centuries, farmers would leave their homesteads during the summer, and move to Thorlákshöfn to fish. It was not unusual for people to have two jobs, and many fishermen have alternative employment to tide them over the periods when they cannot go to sea. Many fishing boats still use this port because it has one of the best harbours in the south.

North of here **Hveragerdi** is one of the country's largest and most famous hot springs areas, particularly useful as it is so close to Reykjavík. The geyser Gryta spouts every 2 hours without fail. Most employment in this area is based around horticulture and there are many greenhouses, which use the natural hot water for heating.

The town is popular with tourists and has a hotel, swimming pool and health resort. The national agricultural college is also sited here. The town can trace its origins back to the founding of a wool processing factory at Reykjafoss in Varmá. The first electric generator to be used east of Hellisheidi was installed at the water falls in 1906. The first greenhouses were erected in 1929 growing a wide range of crops, mostly salad vegetables, but even bananas have been grown. A visit to the Eden Garden Centre, a massive complex housing greenhouses, gift shops and cafés makes a pleasant excursion.

Selfoss is the largest town on the south coast, although in fact it is about 15km (9 miles) inland. It is an industrial and commercial centre, and the centre for one of the most fertile farming districts in the country: it has the largest dairy farm in Iceland. There are good sports facilities, with both an indoor and outdoor pool, a hotel, restaurant, cinema and museums.

The south coast's main harbour for many years was **Eyrarbakki**, and fishing is still the main occupation, although the population is decreasing. One of the country's oldest buildings can be found here, to the east of the church, Húsid built in 1765, is the former home of a Danish merchant. In the town are many old wooden buildings. The beach is noted for its beauty and surf, and it is a good area for bird watching. Another notable beach may be found at **Stokkseyri**, another fishing and agricultural centre. Close to the village there is an interesting folk museum, Rjómabúid.

Hope *monument,*
Grindavík

Tour of the South-West and South, by Car (see maps pages 69 and 105)

Many places in the south and south-west can be visited within a day from Reykjavík if necessary, but there are enough hotels and hostels to allow frequent halts, if so desired.

Follow the main road out of the capital, to a fork as the road climbs up onto Hellisheidi. The road to the right leads down into Ölfus and to Thorlákshöfn. Just before the latter, there is a crossroads. A left turn follows Ölfus Way to rejoin the main road to Hveragerdi. A right turn leads to Selvogur, a curious, sparsely populated area. Strandakirkja at Engilsvík is worth a visit. From Selvogur there is a route back to Reykjavík via the hot springs at Krísuvík and along the shores of Lake Kleifarvatn, or you can continue along the coast to Grindavík.

From the crossroads at Ölfus, it is a straight road to Thorlákshöfn, a fairly young fishing town, with a good harbour, and from where the daily ferry sails to the Vestmannaeyjar (Westman Islands).

From the fork on the lower slopes of Hellisheidi, the main road branches left up Hveradalir over the top of Hellisheidi (374m, 1,227ft) and down to Kambar to Hveragerdi, with its hothouses heated by the thermal springs. Reykir Horticultural College is situated above the river Varmá. There is a hotel, and the unique Eden Garden Centre. Here bananas and other tropical fruits are grown under glass, as well as horticultural and salad crops and flowers.

From Hveragerdi, continue along the main road, skirting the southern slopes of Ingólfsfjall (551m, 1,808ft) and on to Selfoss. The bridge over Ölfusá is quite new, because the original, built in 1891, was destroyed when it collapsed under the weight of two lorries in 1944. Selfoss is a market town and its first house, Tryggvaskáli, built in 1890, is still standing, just east of the bridge. The river Ölfusá with its rapids and deep pools is the pride of the town. There are two filling stations, hospital, campsite, museum and art gallery, swimming pool and supermarket, and two hotels. The Hotel Selfoss has a very good restaurant, and a very noisy Saturday night disco, although it must be said the local youth do not start to party until midnight. It is a good base to explore the area of hot springs to the north of the town, and as it is the last major settlement along the southern coast before Höfn, it is a good idea to stock up with the essentials, especially if you are planning to spend some time at Skaftafell National Park.

South of Selfoss are two fishing villages, Eyrarbakki, which has a well preserved Danish merchant's house, dating back to 1765, and Stokkseyri which has converted an old fisherman's hostel into a museum.

Back over the bridge at Selfoss, towards Reykjavík, a right turn leads past Ingólfsfjall. A left turn at the bridge over Sog goes through Grafningur and west of Lake Thingvallavatn to Thingvellir, via the hydro-electric station at Ljósifoss, and Steingrímsstöd then east of the lake.

Thingvellir is the most historically significant place in Iceland, also the site of the lava gorge of Almannagjá, the waterfall Öxarárfoss, and the old farm and the church, all within easy reach of Hotel Valhöll. In the distance one can see a mountain range. Lake Thingvallavatn is the largest in the country.

From Thingvellir routes lead across Mosfellsheidi to Reykjavík, or east via Gjábakki to Laugarvatn, or north by a mountain road over Uxahryggir to Lundarreykjadalur or through Kaldidalur between Ok and Langjökull to Húsafell in Borgarfjördur in west Iceland.

Along the Grímsnes road from Selfoss is Kerid, which is well worth a visit; a lake in an extinct explosion crater.

A left turn at Svínavatn leads to Laugarvatn with its boarding schools, used for summer hotels, and its natural sauna pools. From Laugarvatn either follow the summer road to Thingvellir via Gjábakki, or drive up Langárdalur, over the river Brúará and on to Gullfoss and Geysir, Iceland's two most celebrated tourist attractions.

Haukadalur, the site of an ancient school, is just north of Geysir. There is a mountain road from Gullfoss which leads north with the Lake Hvítárvatn on the left and Kerlingarfjöll mountain range on the right. There is a summer ski school at Ásgardur in Kerlingarfjöll. The Icelandic Touring Club has a hut there and at Hvítárnes. The road continues up Kjölur between two glaciers, Langjökull and Hofsjökull, to Hveravellir where there is a touring club hut, hot springs and a swimming pool.

Instead of taking the Laugarvatn turn-off, the Grímsnes road near the river Brúará goes to Skálholt, which was a bishop's seat from 1056 to 1784 and for centuries the site of an important school. Recent decades have seen some of its former functions re-established. There is now a church there, and a folk museum. Among the relics from former times is Bishop Páll Jónsson's tomb dating from 1211.

East from Skálholt, a road leads over the river Brúará to join the Skeid-Hreppar road. A little to the west of Skálholt there is the Biskupstungur road which also leads to Geysir and Gullfoss via Aratunga where there is a restaurant open during the summer. East from Selfoss and left on to the Skeid-Hreppar road leads to the Skálholt road, then to the route for Gnúpverjahreppur and Thjórsárdalur. A number of farms were buried in ash during the Hekla eruption of 1104 and one of them, Stöng, has been excavated. Further down the valley, one can see a reconstruction of the same historical farm, Skeljastadir, which was built in 1974, at the time of 1100th anniversary celebrations. The country's largest hydro-electric power station is in Thjórsárdalur at Búrfell (not to be confused with Búrfell near Hafnafjördur). It harnesses the Thjórsá river. There are several beautiful waterfalls in the valley; one of them, Háifoss, is 122m (400ft) high. The road continues up and out of Thjórsárdalur across a fairly new bridge at Sandafell. From there it goes north to the hydro-electric power stations at Sigalda and Hrauneyjarfoss on the river Tungná.

A mountain road runs north across Sigalda, a range of hills on the edge of Sprengisandur. The road goes west of Thórisvatn which, at 70sq km (27sq miles), is the second largest lake in Iceland. There is a wonderful view of the glaciers Vatnajökull, Hofsjökull and Langjökull. The Icelandic Touring Club has a hut on this route which is situated in Nyidalur, south-west of Tungnafellsjökull, at 800m (2,624ft) above sea level. From Nyidalur it is possible to drive to Tómasarhagi, Fjórdungsalda and the north.

At Hreppar, instead of heading for Thjórsárdalur, drive north, crossing the river Stóra-Laxá to Hrunamannahreppur, an administrative district containing the settlements of Hreppholar, Flúdir and Hruni. Flúdir is an excellent place to stop for a meal of magnificent fish served by girls in national costume. There is also a residential school used as a summer hotel. From Flúdir, a road leads to the river Hvítá, which is crossed at Bruárhlöd, and then on a short distance to Gullfoss and Geysir and then back to Reykjavík.

Eastwards along the main road (No 1) is Iceland's longest river, Thjórsá, 230km (143 miles) long. Most of the river's water comes from Hofsjökull. South of Arnarfell, the river branches into several streams which cross a grassy plain known as Thjórsárver, which has the world's largest nesting colony of pink-footed geese. Thjórsá was first bridged in 1895. From here you can drive towards Hekla, the country's most famous volcano. Hekla is surrounded by lava sandmash and pumice. The last major eruption was in 1947-8 but there have been minor eruptions in 1970, 1980 and 1982.

The waterfalls Tröllkonuhlaup and Thjófafoss can be seen on the river Thjórsá near Búrfell, and the striking Fossabrekkur rapids on the river Ytri-Rangá. If Thjórsá is followed north, the road eventually joins the road leading to Sigalda. Before Sigalda is reached, however, a right turn leads to Landmannalaugar. There are hot streams to bathe in and a landscape with an unbelievable range of colours. The Icelandic Touring Club has a hut there and there is a campsite.

The road east from Landmannalaugar, called the North Mountain Road, passes many beauty spots, such as Eldgjá and Ófærufoss. There is another mountain route which travels farther south, nearer the Myrdalsjökull glacier, but it has to be approached from Rangárvellir, via Hvanngil and Maelifellssandur.

Another route is north across the river Tungná from Landmannalaugar and then turn right just south of Thórisvatn. This leads to the Fishing Lakes, Veidivötn, an area of outstanding natural beauty. There is an Icelandic Touring Club hut at Tjaldvatn and it is quite easy

Natural bridge and waterfall at Ófærufoss

to spend a couple of days walking around. There is also a mountain road up to another Icelandic Touring Club hut at Jökulheimar, on the western slopes of Vatnajökull.

The main road east from Vegamót leads to Raudilaekur and then Thykkvibaer, a village which dates back to the early settlers. Just west of the bridge over the Ytri-Rangá there is another farm of historical interest called Aegissída. There are twelve caves under one of the fields, with writing and symbols on the walls that have led some to believe that they were former dwelling places of Irish monks who inhabited Iceland before the arrival of the first Norsemen.

East of the Rangá bridge lies Hella, which has grown steadily since it became a trading centre in 1927. Being a market town, it has a wide range of services including guest house, restaurant and a campsite and it is possible to tour the area on a pony from a trekking centre. East of Hella are the farms Gunnarsholt and Keldur. The former is an experimental farm and plays a leading role in land reclamation projects, while the latter has a farmhouse dating back to 1200, the oldest building in Iceland. The road via these farms is only suitable for four-wheel drive vehicles.

Other interesting places in the Rangárvellir area are the wooded district of Hvannteigur and Oddi, one of the most famous farms in the country's history, where Saemundur the Learned founded his school in the Middle Ages. Saemundur's grandson Jón Loftsson, who died in 1197, was like an uncrowned king.

The next town on the route is Hvolsvöllur, with its restaurant, guest house, campsite and a range of other services. Hvolsvöllur is the business centre for the middle of Rangárvallasysla county, and again agriculture and allied industries is the main employer. From here many places familiar to Saga readers are within driving distance — for example, Hlídarendi, Gunnar Hámundarson's farm. There is an experimental arable farm at Sámsstadir which has specialised in corn growing since 1927, and a tree nursery at Tumastadir, founded in 1947.

Further up the valley is the farm Múlakot with its magnificent tree garden, and many waterfalls. The last farm in the valley has a youth hostel in an old farmhouse. There are also views of the glaciers and the highest mountain peaks in southern Iceland, and the Thórsmörk nature reserve, which has a campsite and hut accommodation. To reach it, drive east from Hvolsvöllur across the bridge over the Markarfljót, and then turn immediately left. There are several difficult rivers to cross on the way, including Krossá. The best way is by organised trip or with your own guide. A mountain road leads east from Fljótshlíd behind the glaciers to Skaftafellssysla. It is the continuation of the Thorsmörk road and is only suitable for four-wheel drive vehicles. The whole of this area is of interest to the backpacker or long distance walker, and there are interesting routes to Landmannalaugar and to Skógar, via Fimmvörduháls.

East of the main road from Markarfljót bridge, there is Eyjafjallajökull on the left and flat farmland on the right. This road leads to the waterfalls Gljúfrabúi and Seljalandsfoss, and another excellent place to stop. Nearby are caves which feature in the legends of Iceland, and one of them, near Fit Farm, is mentioned in the story of Anna from Stóruborg. Another is called Steinahellir, a short distance east of Holtsós. There is an open-air swimming pool at Seljavellir, fed from a warm spring. Travelling along the foot of the mountains, through fertile farmland, one comes to the village of Skógar, with its summer hotel and magnificent waterfall, Skógarfoss. There is a local museum here and swimming pool. East from the village, an area of black volcanic sands is soon reached. To the north is Sólheimajökull glacier, and to the south, the Atlantic.

As you drive across the river Jökulsá, there is a smell of sulphur in the air, an ever present reminder of the area's volcanic activity. East of Jökulsá, is Vestur-Skaftafellssysla, and more fertile country with the island of Pétursey, literally rising from the sand, on the right. There is a turn-off for the nature reserve at Dyrhólaey, and on the right, is a causeway on to the island itself. The view is staggering, with a sheer drop of 120m (400ft) from the top of the island down to the sea. The island (which literally means 'door-hole') gets its name from the massive arch that the sea has eroded from the headland. There is a lighthouse on the island, built in 1926. East along the main road, the valley is reached by crossing the mountain ridge. At the other side of the ridge is Reynisfjall mountain which must be crossed to get to Vík í Myrdal. If instead the route south into Reynishverfi is taken, the most southerly farm in Iceland at Gardar can be visited. On the beach there are interesting caves and basalt formations to see.

From Reynishverfi, the road leads to Vík, the only town in Vestur-Skaftafell county, which has a campsite, guest house, sleeping bag accommodation, summer houses and a number of services: from Vík, the road goes east past Víkurhamrar cliffs and out into the vast black Myrdal Sands, 700sq km (270sq miles) of sands washed down from the Katla eruptions. On a good day, the view stretches all the way to Vatnajökull. (The southernmost point of Iceland is Kötlutangi 15km (9 miles) to the east of Vík.) Once across the sands, the lavafield created in the Laki eruption of 1783 is reached. At 565sq km (218sq miles), this was the largest lava-flow recorded in historical times anywhere in the world.

From here it is only a short drive to Kirkjubaejarklaustur, where there is a hotel, restaurant, campsite and other tourist facilities. A short distance up the Skaftá river is Eldmessutangi, the point where the lava-flow stopped in the 1783 eruption, during the famous Fire Mass. Before the reformation there was a convent at Kirkjubaejar-klaustur. There is a mountain road up to the Laki crater and many fine examples of columnar basalt may be seen.

From Kirkjubaejarklaustur, the route east is both beautiful and varied. There is a waterfall and interesting basalt formations at Dvergshamrar, and an attractive seventeenth-century turf church at Núpsstadur. It is here that the southern region ends; across Skeidarársandur the region leads into east Iceland. Ahead, the highest peak in the country, Hvannadalshnjúkur, at 2,119m (6,952ft), rises out of Öraefajökull glacier and then you are in Skaftafell National Park.

3

THE SOUTH
AND SKAFTAFELL

The south of Iceland is dominated by the huge plain that sprawls, in places many miles wide, to the southern edge of Vatnajökull, Europe's largest glacier. The area is predominantly concerned with agriculture and associated industries, although there are a few fishing villages along the coast. It is criss-crossed by rivers, both freshwater and glacial, and there are many lakes.

It is always difficult to decide where the region starts, but having visited Thingvellir, Geysir and Gullfoss, the area known as the Southern Lands reaches from Reykjanes to Vatnajökull.

The ring road is a good metalled road — with just the occasional pot hole — until just about 9km (5½ miles) beyond Hvolsvöllur. It then becomes a gravel surface and you have to concentrate hard on your driving. Although there is a maximum speed limit of 50km/h (30mph) in urban areas, 70km/h (40mph) in rural areas and 80-90km/h (50-60mph) on highways, the visitor is not likely to come near these speeds until he or she has built up a bit of confidence. The gravel roads, especially in the early summer, can still be potholed and cracked after the winter. Boulders often lie strewn across the road, and there is the damage of stones being thrown up from vehicles in front. Dust is another problem, and in the summer months you can normally spot another vehicle on the road miles away because of the dust cloud it throws up. All drivers in Iceland use dipped headlights at all times, and because of the dirt, most filling stations have free high-powered water jets so that you can clean off your vehicles, especially the lights.

The drive from Holt, through Skógar to Vikand then on to Kirkjubaejarklaustur, up round Kúdafljót, and across Eldhraun, is incredible. Then you have to cross another lunar desert landscape, skirting to the north of Skeidaráesandur to Skaftafell.

The glacier fingers from Myrdalsjökull creep down on your left, and the ice is blacked by the lava sand it has picked up. Stop for a few moments by the river Jökulsá in the summer and listen to the almost incessant calls of birds — curlew, redshank and oystercatchers and others.

The road now passes very close to the sea and the towering cliffs play host to tens of thousands of sea birds, particularly large colonies of gannets. After the lava desert and Kirkjubaejarklaustur, the road follows the southern slopes of a number of mountain ranges. In many areas, sheltered from the north and easterly winds, clusters of trees huddle in the valleys, and everywhere along this route there are spectacular waterfalls cascading down the cliffs. At Skiedarár there is a very long single lane wooden bridge, with passing points at convenient intervals, and then it is only a short drive to the green oasis of Skaftafell.

Distances take longer than you expect, because you have to negotiate around pot holes, especially if you are not driving a four-wheel drive vehicle. It is just when your confidence starts to build up, and you put your foot down a little, that you hit the biggest pot hole on the road. On even rougher stretches of road, and there are miles upon miles of them, it is easy to upset the tracking of the vehicle because of the constant battering. It is worth having this checked out at the first opportunity, because if the tracking is bad you will be sliding all over some of the mud tracks, especially after wet weather, and even in a four-wheel vehicle.

The south is the most extensive area of lowland in the country, flanked by the sea on one side and mountains and glaciers on the other. In places the mountains are simply ridges that run for several hundred yards, and they are reminiscent of an American western landscape. The walls of these mesas are very steep and there are many spectacular waterfalls. Because there are so many faults in the rocks, it is quite common to see a raging torrent of water pouring out

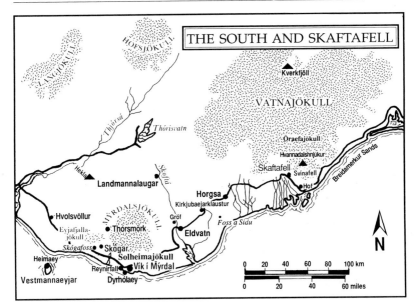

THE SOUTH AND SKAFTAFELL

of a cave several hundred feet above the ground before it plunges down into a pool or river below.

Off the coast you can see the Vestmannaeyjar (Westman Islands) which had to be evacuated in 1973 when an eruption took place. Still further out to sea is the island of Surtsey, born of a submarine eruption in 1963 which lasted for more than 2 years.

There are many villages in the southern plains, and a comprehensive road network so travelling is easy. Progress is more difficult, but infinitely more rewarding, when vehicles are left behind, and a journey on foot is undertaken in the Skaftafell, one of Iceland's greenest areas, and now one of the country's three national parks. It is strange to walk in this oasis with the sea on one side and the Öraefajökull glacier behind. There are many walks both in the park and, with a guide, up on the glacier.

In the west of the region there are many geothermal areas, including the district known as 'Greenhouses' because the earth's hot water is used to heat glass-houses. The country's largest hydro-electric stations are also to be found in this region.

A most surprising fact is that Skaftafell had hardly any visitors

Waterfall outside a campsite near Kirkjubaejarklaustur

Foss a Sidu east of Kirkjubaejarklaustur

before 1974, because it was so difficult to reach. It was not until 1974 that the final stretch of the national highway around the country was completed to commemorate the 1,100th anniversary of the country's first settlement. Before then, roads were built across the southern plains, but they were often washed away by the ice melt and floodwater coming down from the mountains and glaciers. Now, the road is elevated in places to allow the floodwater to pass underneath, and buses regularly visit the park; and Skaftafell, once a mystery, is now known and loved by thousands of visitors from both home and abroad. The journey across the great sands and rivers to get to the park is also unforgettable.

Ingólfshöfdi, on the edge of the region, is named after Iceland's first settler Ingólfur Arnarson, who spent his first winter there. It is a cliff which stands alone in a vast area of sand, close to the sea and about 10km (6.2 miles) from Fagurhólsmyri. The cliffs play host to thousands of nesting sea birds and it is possible to get very close to them. Kirkjubaejarklaustur is one of the largest farms in Skaftafell and a small village has grown up there recently. There is plenty to see including Kirkjuhólar, the remains of an old convent, and Systrastapi, which is an overhanging cliff to the west of the village. There is another cliff at **Hjörleifshöfdi** which can be climbed. The views from the top are stunning.

Mount Reynisfjall, 340m (1,115ft) high, is near Vík in Myrdalur. There is a road which goes up to the top of the mountain, where there is a long-range radar navigation station. This is another good place for views and photographs. There are some unusual stone pillars called Reynisdrangar at the seaward foot of the mountain.

Not far away to the west is **Dyrhólaey**. It has a huge cliff overhanging the ocean, which has a hole in it. Large boats can pass through this hole in good weather. Nearby **Hekla**, at 1,491m (4,892ft), is Iceland's most famous volcano. Its first recorded eruption was in 1104; since then it has erupted fifteen times, the last time in 1982. In March 1947 when it erupted the column rose to 30,000m (100,000ft) while the lava flow covered 65sq km (25sq miles).

The country's largest electrical plant is near Búrfell, and there is another to the north at Sigalda.

Landmannalaugar is a beautiful dale between the mountains and is a very popular tourist spot in the summer. It must be remembered that it takes only a few people to constitute a crowd in Iceland's beauty spots. Visitors can take advantage of the hot pools and there

PLACES OF INTEREST IN THE SOUTH

Búrfell
Waterfalls Tröllkonuhlaup and Thjófafoss on the river Thjórsá, plus the striking rapids of Fossabrekkur on the river Ytri-Rangá. (Not to be confused with Búrfell in Hafnarfjördur.)

Eyjafjöll
Impressive mountain range north-west of Vík with two remarkable waterfalls, Skógarfoss and Seljalandsfoss. There are several caves including Paradísarhellir (Paradise Cave).

Hekla
Iceland's most famous volcano, north-west of Myrdalsjökull.

Ingólfshöfdi
A huge cliff south of Vatnajökull; the resting site of thousands of sea birds.

Landmannalaugar
Beautiful dale in the mountains east of Búrfell.

Mount Reynisfjall
Accessible by road from Vík. It is 340m (1,115ft) high and there are impressive views from the top.

Thjórsárver
South of Arnarfell, home of the world's largest nesting colony of pink-footed geese.

Thórsmörk
North of Eyjafjallajökull. Considered by Icelanders to be one of the country's most beautiful spots.

Vestmannaeyjar
(Westman Islands)
Off the south coast, including Surtsey, which rose from the sea in 1963. Heimaey, the largest island has the country's largest fishing fleet, an airport, marine zoo and folk museum. The islands teem with birdlife.

is a rest house.

Eyjafjöll is a beautiful mountain range capped by the Eyjafjallajökull glacier, which is 1,660m (5,446ft) high. There are many waterfalls, the most remarkable of which are Skógarfoss and Seljalandsfoss. There are also caves which can be explored including Hrútshellir by Hrutafell, and Paradísarhellir, which literally means Paradise Cave. The valley is beautiful and so unspoilt that is has often been used by film companies, especially those making films

Basalt cliffs and stacks at Dyrhólaey

A boat trip around the Westman Islands

about prehistoric times. There is also an open swimming pool in the mountains, only accessible by a steep pass. A cliff forms one side of the pool.

Thórsmörk can only be reached by four-wheel drive vehicles, or trucks, but the journey is worth it. Icelanders consider it to be one of their most beautiful places, but care is necessary. The journey can only be made when water levels are low, and many cars have been swept away when unsuspecting motorists tried to ford the rivers, not appreciating how strong the currents are. It is best to ask a guide to take you to visit this lovely place.

There are many historical places in the Rangárvallasysla district, including **Hlídarendi** in Fljótshlid and **Bergthórshvoll** in Landeyjar, both of which are dramatic settings for the *Njálasaga*. To the north of Eyjafjallajökull glacier is **Basar**, a weird and beautiful place.

Heimaey is the largest of the **Vestmannaeyjar** (Westman Islands), the group of islands off the southern coast of Iceland, and has the country's largest fishing fleet. Most of the 5,000 inhabitants are engaged in fishing, fish processing or associated industries, although tourism is also now an important industry.

The massive eruption in 1973 began here; it lasted until May and half the town was submerged in lava while the rest was covered with ash and dust. For 5 months the community fought to halt the advance of the lava. High pressure hoses poured millions and millions of gallons of sea water on to the leading edge of the advancing lava in a bid to cool it down and divert it. By a miracle the 5m (16ft) high lava wall stopped only yards from the island's hospital which was saved, although several feet of ash had to be swept from its flat roof. Less fortunate was a house close to the hospital. The lava wall stopped halfway through the house and the remainder can still be seen poking from the towering wall of black lava. The harbour and fish processing plants were also undamaged and within a few weeks most of the population had returned to clean up and continue their lives. About 400 houses were buried or destroyed by fire.

The harbour and factories were not damaged because of the ingenuity of Icelandic scientists, who used cold sea water to slow down the advance of the lava. The sea water was pumped into the approaching lava flow, and miraculously it stopped. The eruption not only extended the size of the island, it produced an enormous amount of lava which has been utilized for building and road making.

Heimaey has an airport and there are regular flights from

Reykjavík. It is possible to fly to Heimaey early in the morning, spend a day touring the island and then return to Reykjavík in the early evening. Some return air fares also include the cost of a guided tour on the island and this is well worth taking. You can visit the puffin colonies; the birds nest not only on the cliffs but on the grass banks as well.

One of the national 'sports' on the island is to swing from a rope hanging from the top of the cliff, seeing how many eggs you can take from the puffins' nests. Both the eggs and the birds are eaten on the island. Heimaey has a hotel, cafés, cinema, hospital, and a sports centre with a swimming pool. There is also a marine zoo and a folk museum.

Skaftafell and Glacier Country

Although the north of Iceland has enormous beauty, especially the areas around Lake Myvatn, the national park of Skaftafell and the glacier country beyond is considered by many to be the most attractive region. It appeals because it offers everything the outdoor enthusiast wants. There are magnificent panoramas, walks of varying degrees of difficulty, and the most breathtaking views. In Skaftafell there is always the backdrop of the glaciers and up on the ice, one has the sensation of entering another world. Skaftafell has been a national park since 1967 and it was created with the help of the World Wildlife Fund.

The glaciers have a silent power. They move relentlessly onwards and can crush everything in their path. Yet, when actually standing on them, there is a sense of enormous peace and tranquillity. Ice climbing is great fun though it can be dangerous and should not be undertaken unless experienced. There is enormous satisfaction in being able to climb, spider-like, up a vertical cliff face with just ice-axes and crampons for grip.

Then there are the walks over some of the most spectacular countryside in Iceland, where in the summer the greenness of it all is breathtaking. Skaftafell is an oasis in a desert of sand, and is the more spectacular because of this. It is less than $3\frac{1}{2}$ hours by coach from Reykjavík, and should not be missed.

It is possible to camp at Skaftafell and there is a shop and warden service throughout the summer; camping is really the only way to see the national park and experience it properly. There is a marvellous feeling in being able to wake up in this huge area of spectacular

Skógarfoss

Horgsa

countryside, with only the birds above for company. Even in the height of summer, the park rarely gets busy, and the campsite is large enough to allow everyone their privacy. The buses between Höfn and Reykjavík have a stopover in Skaftafell because there is now a filling station and café. For campers the weather forecast is posted daily in Icelandic and English, and the shop sells large-scale maps of the area. There is a full time warden in the park to help with any problems or enquiries, and there are charts available to help you identify the flora and fauna of the region. Bed and breakfast accommodation is quite new to Iceland, but a number of farmers now offer it, and a farm at Bólti, clearly signposted at Skaftafell, offers rooms if you want a few home comforts.

This part of Iceland also encompasses the most accessible parts of the glacier country. The district is known as **Öraefasveit**. It comprises the foot of the Öraefajökull glacier which forms the southern part of **Vatnajökull**, the largest ice-cap in Europe, and the fertile strip that runs between the mountains and the coast. The word Öraefasveit comes from *sveit* which means a district, and *öraefi* which means an uninhabited wasteland. There are no ports or natural harbours along this shore, and the waves of the Atlantic pound it relentlessly, which could also account for part of the district's name.

Although the glaciers and ice-covering on Öraefasveit give an impression of cold, there is enormous power and turbulence just below the surface. Not for nothing is this area also called 'The Land of Fire'. **Öraefajökull** is a typical cone volcano and it has erupted more than once since Iceland was first settled in the ninth century. The last recorded eruption was in 1727 when it did considerable damage to stock and killed large numbers of animals trapped in the lava-flow. But it was the massive explosion of 1362 that did the most damage, and devastated the entire region. Almost all the existing farmsteads here were wiped out, and a gigantic pillar of volcanic ash killed off all the vegetation, which meant that farmers could not return for many years. Records show that before this massive eruption there were six churches and at least twenty-four farms, whereas now there are only eight farmsteads and one church.

There are many rivers flowing through this region from the glaciers and mountains to the sea, and because of the intensity of the flood waters they are constantly changing their course. Due to this, engineers found it extremely difficult to complete the road around Iceland. Every time a section across this southern plain was com-

THINGS TO SEE IN SKAFTAFELL

Glaciers
Vatnajökull is the largest ice-cap in Europe.

Gröf
Old farmhouse excavated from the pumice which covered it in 1362.

Hof
Turf-roofed church.

Hvannadalshnjúkur
Highest peak in Iceland, best climbed from Sandfell. It is 2,119m (6,952ft) high and situated to the south of Vatnajökull.

Skaftafell National Park
Created in 1967 with help from the World Wildlife Fund. A rich haven of flora and fauna. Wardens on duty in the summer months. Campsite with shop, café and toilet facilities.

Svartifoss
Waterfall flowing over columnar basalt formations.

pleted flood waters washed it away.

The Öraefajökull glacier is not always visible; frequently it is hidden behind the mountains, but its presence is always felt. In places tongues of the glacier advance quite close to the road, often forming deep lagoons in which trapped icebergs bob about. Such a lake can be seen on the river Jökulsá, near the Breidamerkur sands (see also chapter 4). This river was only bridged in 1967 and although it is less than one mile long, the river holds more water than many others which are much longer. The lagoon formed where it swells out is well over 90m (300ft) deep in places. At the farm of Svínafell in the west, the glacier encroaches almost to the door, although like most others in recent years, it has started to recede.

The mountains consist mainly of volcanic tuff, although the rocks do contain a number of semi-precious stones such as opal, jasper, and Iceland spar.

The fertile grasslands of Öraefasveit are used mainly for cattle and sheep farming, although two or three centuries ago they were covered in the typical squat Icelandic brushwood. The slow advance of the glaciers and the constant overgrazing by sheep, however, killed off most of these woodlands, although areas still exist in and

Heimaey

On the road, Svínafell, east of Skaftafell

Road bridge at Eldvatn (picture taken after 10pm)

near the Skaftafell park.

The whole of this coastline is warmed by the Gulf Stream and this part of the country has one of the mildest climates in Iceland. Although it gets quite high rainfall, there is little snow and ice, and few frosts. The average temperature in January has for a number of years been above freezing and this special climate, especially in the summer, has led to a unique vegetation, especially in Skaftafell and Svínafell. Many plants and ferns, not found in any other part of Iceland, can be found growing in the national park, right at the very edge of the glacier.

In the sea to the south of Skaftafell, seals can be seen, and they are often hunted by the local farmers who see the pelts as a valuable addition to their incomes. Polar bears are reputed to have come ashore in Iceland in this area, having been swept across on ice floes from Greenland. There is a report of a polar bear being killed by farmers in this region in 1748. However, the only animal likely to be seen is the arctic fox, although there are hundreds of thousands of sea birds, the most common of which are puffins, fulmar, arctic tern, razorbill and oystercatcher. Beware of the fulmar, it has some very nasty habits. If its nesting site is approached too closely, or the bird is upset, it is likely to disgorge the oily, fishy contents of its stomach over the offender. After several baths the smell may be eliminated from the skin, but no matter how many times the affected clothes are cleaned, the smell will linger on. The largest breeding ground of the ferocious arctic skua in the northern hemisphere is on the Breida-merkur sands (see chapter 4). It is a rapacious predator attacking other birds and their young, and stealing their eggs. The area is also interesting because it is on the migration route for a number of birds in the autumn and spring.

Apart from its present day interest as a national park, Skaftafell is also important because of the part it played in Iceland's history. It used to be the meeting place for the region's assembly and it is mentioned many times in the island's Sagas. Flosi, one of the characters in the *Njálasaga*, used to live at Svínafell, while another, Kári Sólmundarson, lived at a now abandoned farm at Breidá. Until the introduction of air flights, much of this region was truly isolated, almost the only communication with the outside world coming from the occasional freighters which plied along the coast. For centuries, the sturdy Icelandic horse was not only the pack animal but also the only way of travelling long distances. A few intrepid travellers would venture into this region on horseback but it could be a hazardous journey.

Because of the lack of good anchorages, the freighters would often try to unload their cargoes on the ice floes, or some way out to sea. The coast has many wrecks to show how dangerous this could be. A Dutch cargo vessel is reported to have foundered off this coast in 1667 with a valuable cargo on board, but all attempts to find her have failed. Although the name Iceland is a misnomer, as ice does not cover much of the countryside, anyone visiting the country must see the glaciers.

It is from this region that the best approaches to Öraefajökull and Vatnajökull can be made. Although there are many legends of islanders crossing the glacier from north to south, the first recorded crossing was in 1875 by the British explorer W.L. Watts. The first organised all-Iceland crossing was completed by three young men from Höfn in 1926. Since 1954 the Icelandic Geological Society has made many trips on to the glaciers, and travel has been made much easier by the use of snowmobiles.

The ascent of **Hvannadalshnjúkur**, the highest peak in Iceland at 2,119m(almost 7,000ft), is best attempted fromSandfell, an abandoned farm. At least 6 hours must be allowed for the reasonably fit, and May and June are considered the best months for climbing.

It is strongly advisable not to climb glaciers alone unless experienced. There are hundreds of crevices and cracks crisscrossing the glacier and it is very easy to become cut off. For instance, just after World War II, an American plane crashed into the glacier, and half the passengers and crew were killed outright. The remainder were unscathed and started to make their way down the glacier to safety. Not one of them survived, and the glacier continued to throw their bodies up at its feet for years afterwards.

It is possible to hire caravanettes and the like, or to stay in a neighbouring town, but the time taken to drive to the park each day cuts down the time left for sightseeing.

Perhaps the contrasts make Skaftafell so exciting. There is the roaring Atlantic on one side, and the vast white mass of the glacier on the other, and in between these, a paradise of lush grasses and flowers.

There are many walks in and around Skaftafell and most of them are well marked, not only with distances but also with the approximate times needed to complete them. It is possible to walk up to the

The mouth of an ice cave
Kverkfjöll mountains

Hveradalir in the
Kverkfjöll mountains

A view from the Kverkfjöll mountains

base of the Kristínartindar peaks, which rise to about 1,130m (3,700ft), or down into the glacial valley of Morsárdalur. Another walk goes to Baejarstadaskógur, a veritable forest by Icelandic standards of willows, birches and rowans. One has to cross some rivers, and while it can be done by four-wheel drive vehicle, it is much more of an adventure to hike in.

There are wardens on duty throughout the summer months to advise on how best to see the park, and the campsite has a modern toilet block with washrooms and showers, a shop and café. Maps and guides of the park can be bought there.

Worth visiting while in the park is the **Svartifoss** waterfall, about half a mile from the three farms. The columnar basalt formations are said to have inspired the interior décor of the National Theatre in Reykjavík.

Two other places of interest to visit are **Hof** and **Kvisker** with its many rare flowers. *Hof* is the Icelandic word for 'temple' and you will see it cropping up on the map in several places. Hof used to be the site of a pagan temple but there is now a turf-roofed church, rebuilt in the 1880s. It can be inspected as can Gröf, an old farm that has been excavated from the pumice which covered it during the 1362 eruption. Kvisker is a resting post for travellers, especially in olden days for those on horseback.

4

THE SOUTH-EAST AND THE EASTERN FJORDS

The drive past Skaftafell leads into the south-east corner of Iceland. Behind is Europe's largest glacier and one of the world's most fascinating places. For although the ground is covered with ice in the hills, underneath the volcanoes still rumble on. Occasionally the heat rises close enough to the surface to melt the ice, and massive torrents of water sweep down across the plain into the sea. It was this kind of tidal wave, of greater volume than the Amazon estuary, that would frequently sweep away roads and bridges. Now, the road has been built to take you across the sand and flood plain, and beyond, to fishing towns like Höfn, and the east coast.

The horses of this region are reputed to be the most sturdy in Iceland, and they were nicknamed the 'water horses' because of their ability to cross the toughest ground, including fast-flowing rivers.

The whole of this region is still very active geologically speaking and it is possible to see how the country has, and is, being formed. Almost all the inhabited areas of Iceland, that is the coastal plains running between sea and mountain, were once covered by the oceans. The original coastline can still be spotted in many areas along the foothills of the mountains in the south-east.

About 10,000 years ago, the glaciers melted from the lowlands, and the island literally began to rise from the sea. Geologists think

On the ring road, between Skaftafell and Höfn, near Fell

that the weight of the glaciers was so immense that it physically forced the island down. Proof of this can still be seen on the Hoffellsjökull glacier, near Höfn, which has been known to reveal sea shells from time to time, giving glimpses of its past. Eventually the upward movement of the land ceased, and the south-east corner began to sink back into the sea. At this south-east corner the land is thought to have submerged by as much as 5m (18ft), but this has to be balanced against the constant flow of silt from the glaciers which is extending the area of land around estuaries and in the fjords.

It is possible to fly to Höfn which saves a considerable amount of time, although the drive along the south coast from Reykjavík is an adventure. The road from Skaftafell, for example, to Hof is very potholed and care needs to be taken although it is quite passable by two-wheel drive vehicles. Most drivers try to stick to the centre of the road unless there is oncoming traffic, because the sides of the road can often be washed away, or the verges are soft and you may get stuck. The road deteriorates even more around Hof and you will be lucky to do more than 15-20km/h (9-12mph), so bear this in mind when trying to work out timings. There are incredible rock formations to your left, and the cloud ceiling can drop very quickly, obscuring everything in a blanket of mist. Inland, Öraefajökull dominates the landscape, with its peaks of Hvannadalshnjúkur (2,119m, 6,950ft) — the highest in Iceland — and Snaebreid (2,041m, 6,694ft), but these are often hidden by clouds.

From Hof, the gravel road follows the coast north-eastwards the 100km (62 miles) or so to Höfn, crossing the Breidamerkur sands which stretch for 25km (15 miles), and pass the spectacular finger glacier of Kvíarjökull, and then Fjallsjökull and Breidamerkurjökull.

The photographic possibilities in this area are tremendous, and it is a great place to get out and explore on foot. There are a number of walks in this area and you can discover many lakes formed by the glacier. The two best lakes are both near the road and you can drive right down to their edge. You will jump on the brakes when you first see Breidárlon with its icebergs and intense blue water, but don't take too much film, because the next lake, Jókulsárlón, is much bigger and far more spectacular. The glacier plunges into the water and the huge chunks of ice that break free and drift away are an amazing assortment of colours. Some are pure white, others black because of the lava sand they have collected, others are striped and yet more are vivid blue because of the way they reflect the sun's rays. Many of the

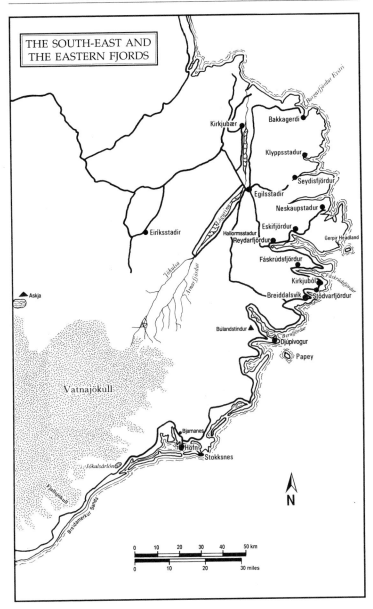

THE SOUTH-EAST AND
THE EASTERN FJORDS

Borgarfjördur Eystri

Kirkjubær

Bakkagerdi

Klyppsstadur

Seydisfjördur

Egilsstadir

Neskaupstadur

Eskifjördur

Eiríksstadir

Hallormsstadur

Reydarfjördur

Gerpir Headland

Fáskrúdsfjördur

Lagarfljot

Jökulsa

Fáskrúdsfjördur

Kirkjuból

Breiddalsvík

Stödvarfjördur

Askja

Jökulsa

Arnarfjördur

Búlandstindur

Berufjördur

Djúpivogur

Papey

Vatnajökull

Bjarnanes

Höfn

Stokksnes

Jökulsárlón

Fjallsjökull

Breidamerkur Sandur

N

| 0 | 10 | 20 | 30 | 40 | 50 km |

| 0 | 10 | 20 | 30 miles |

icebergs have been trapped in the lake for years, while a few drift away out to sea. The sight is so spectacular that a local fisherman in Höfn now offers boat trips round the lake.

The gravel road then skirts the southern flanks of Sudursveit until it reaches the radio station at Smyrlabjórg. From here until Höfn, apart from a 4km (2½ miles) section around Bjarnanes, the road is metalled and fast. Suddenly the vegetation improves, there is rich farmland again with lots of cows, sheep and horses in the fields during the summer months, and then the road swings round Hornafjördur and you drop down into **Höfn**.

There is still a lot of building going on. The youth hostel is well signposted, although a bit of a walk from the bus stop. There is a campsite on the edge of town with washing and toilet facilities, but it can be very windy here so pick your site carefully. At the entrance to the campsite there is an information centre, and people using the campsite can use the shower and bathing facilities at the nearby swimming pool. There is also a large Hotel Edda on the outskirts of the town, a good hotel which is being extended, supermarkets, shops, restaurants, filling stations, cinema and a museum. There is a pharmacist and facilities for hiring cars and horses.

The Höfn airstrip is very close to the town, which is the largest in this south-east corner. Höfn is a thriving fishing port with associated industries such as fish processing. It is also the commercial and market town for a prosperous agriculture inland. In the last few years the town has grown rapidly, again thanks to the completion of the road linking it with towns to the west in 1974. Although it can be a bumpy and long journey there is a regular bus service between Reykjavík and Höfn, and you can stop off on the way to spend a night or two camped out in Skaftafell before continuing your journey. In Iceland, bus schedules are remarkably well adhered to.

Near the airport is Bjarnanes, a very old parsonage and manor that has many close links with the island's history in the Middle Ages. From the Stapahólar hills, just to the south of Bjarnanes, there is a view across the fjord Hornafjördur, to the surrounding mountains and glaciers. Like most other places in Iceland, the photographs almost take themselves, regardless of the quality of the photographer. On 2 August 1924, a plane piloted by the Swedish-American Nelson, who had flown to Iceland in 8½ hours from the Orkney Islands on his way west, landed at Höfn on the final stage of its journey. It was the first plane ever to fly around the world.

Fjallsjökull is one of many fingers of ice that descend towards the low-
lying coastal fringe around Vatnajökull

There are many things to see and do in Höfn, and there is a comfortable modern hotel to stay in as well as a youth hostel, campsite, and guesthouses. Since the road was built in 1974 linking Höfn to the rest of the south coast, there has been a massive increase in the number of travellers. The town used to get intrepid visitors in the past, but they had to arrive by steamer, on horseback, or after a long journey along the north coast and then down the east side of the country. Today, you can fly, or catch a scheduled bus. There are also many tours which take in Höfn and allow further exploration.

The area is good for walking and camping, and immensely attractive to naturalists. There are roads leading northwards to the Eastern Fjords and westwards to Öraefi. There is plenty of good sport available in the area, good cheap fishing in the lakes and rivers, and large numbers of plaice and flounders to catch in the fjords. Traditional Icelandic fishermen work here, using both nets and spears to catch the fish.

There is a greater variety of birdlife here than anywhere else in Iceland. The area is of special interest to ornithologists because many birds, swept in from western Europe on freak winds, have their first chance of landfall on this south-east outcrop of land. About forty species of birds from western Europe have been seen here in recent years, and it is thought that some species from mainland and northern Europe have established themselves in Iceland in this way. Certainly the starling and lapwing first settled and bred here before moving to colonise other parts of the island. The eider breeds in Hornafjördur and there are also large numbers of great skuas, great black-back gulls, fulmars, and arctic terns.

The area is also rich in plant life, and again, many species can be found here which do not appear elsewhere in Iceland. Flora such as the blue sesleria, the rosa dumalis and the green spleenwort can be found. Some of these species can only be found in Öraefi, but the locals, especially the farmers, have always taken a keen interest in the natural history of their area. It is true that until recently much of this region had not been scientifically explored, so new species are being discovered, not because they are new, but because they have not previously been catalogued.

From Höfn it is possible either to walk or to drive to the Almannaskard Pass, which is 11km (7 miles) away, and from here there are magnificent views of the coastline, glaciers and settlements. To the east of the pass there is the deeply indented Papafjördur with the

PLACES OF INTEREST
IN THE SOUTH-EAST

Almannaskard Pass
Seven miles north-east of Höfn. Magnificent views of the coastline, glaciers and settlements.

Breidamerkur Sands
South-west of Höfn. The glaciers almost reach the sea. Farms separated by mud and glacial silt alleged to be the most impressive in the world. Large lagoon on Jökulsá river often containing huge icebergs.

Hallormsstadur
Government forestry centre. Forest trees include spruce and larch, but many other varieties are being planted. Because this is the only major forest in Iceland, many visitors travel to the area.

Höfn
Situated to the south-east of Vatnajökull and virtually cut off until recently. An area rich in wildlife and rare plants. Excellent fishing available. A greater variety of birdlife here than anywhere else in Iceland.

Húsey
Seal colony. There is a youth hostel and horse riding available from the nearby farm.

Skriduklaustur
Experimental farm on site of a fifteenth-century monastery. Part of the buildings now forms a local folk museum.

Stokksnes
US Radar Station, many seals visit off the coast.

estuary of the Papós. When the Norsemen first arrived in Iceland, they landed in this south-east corner, although it was to be several years before the first Norse settler Ingólfur Arnarson made his way along the coast to build his house on the site on which Reykjavík now stands. From the records of these earliest times it was clear that the first settlers on the island were Irish monks, who had chosen to live hermits' lives in the caves along the southern coast, but were gradually driven out by the heathens. It is not known where they went, but they left behind many artefacts, and there are still traces of their presence to be found in some of the place names. Some way north of the Hamarsfjördur, there has been a find that has still to be satisfactorily explained: three Roman coins, all dating from about AD300 were excavated from a field. There are no records of the

Lake Jókulsárlón

Romans being here, but it is possible that a Roman ship, caught up in one of the terrible storms that sweep the area, may have been driven ashore, and some of its crew or at least some of its cargo, landed. Another theory is that the coins were brought in by the Vikings, who would certainly have had access to them during their raids in Britain and the Low Countries. However, no one really knows.

Farther around the coast is the US radar station at **Stokksnes**, which seems to attract all the seals in the area, of which there are large numbers.

There is much of interest to the geologist in this part of the country. The volcanic and glacial rocks contain many precious minerals, notably jasper and opal, and there are many sub-species of rock which are peculiar to Iceland.

The road out of Höfn heading for Djúpivogur is lovely if the weather is fine, but can be hazardous if it is wet or there is a mist. The road follows the sea and hugs the mountains which tower above you on the right-hand side. There are many tight bends and in places, there is a sheer drop down to the sea. Massive scree slopes tower above you on the mountain side, and there are frequent landslides which throw debris across the road. The road is potholed and in wet weather can be very muddy, so drive at a safe speed to avoid sliding about.

Because of the deep fjords which penetrate well inland, you can eat up the miles getting to the various towns. It is a little frustrating when you turn a headland and can see the settlement you are driving to just a few kilometres across the water, but know that you have to drive 50km (30 or so miles) or more to get to it. Throughout the Eastern Fjords almost all the roads hug the coastline. There are a few roads through the mountains which can save you miles, but not necessarily time if the weather is bad. Always check before heading off for a mountain road. Ask the locals what the weather is like and what conditions you will face.

As you head towards Djúpivogur there is the sand bar enclosing Lónsfjördur, the waters of which provide the summer home for hundreds of whooper swans. Once round the headland which skirts Snjotindur, you can see the even larger sand bank that nearly encircles Álftafjördur, with **Djúpivogur** in the distance on a promontory sticking out to sea.

As you approach the settlement, you will see the wooden fish racks where mostly cod are hung out to dry. These racks are a feature all along the coast, a sign that the population is so dependent on the sea for much of its living. It is one of the oldest trading centres in the region and once served a huge area. The oldest house dates back to the arrival of Danish merchants in the area, around the end of the eighteenth century. The town has always prospered because of its good natural harbour. Fishing is the main industry and there is a large freezer plant.

It is also nice to see the trees just outside the town, and because this vegetation is relatively scarce on the island, great pains are taken to protect them. This often includes surrounding them with barbed wire to prevent the sheep from stripping off the bark.

Back westwards along the coast from Höfn there is a change in the geology, and a return to volcanic tuff. The change occurs about 87km (54 miles) from Höfn on the river Jökulsá on the **Breidamerkur sands** (see also chapter 3). Here, glaciers constantly encroach and there is only a narrow strip between mountains and sea. In places the plain is only 5km (3 miles) wide and all the farms are separated by the mud and glacial silt deposits which are said to be more impressive here than anywhere else in the world.

There are many interesting places to visit such as the Hestgerdislón lagoon, just to the south of the Borgarhafnarfjall mountain. Many of the nearby place names are connected with the sea or fishing, reflecting the region's past. Until the end of the sixteenth century there was a small fishing port here known as Hálsar, but due to land subsidence, boats have not been able to use it since. There are also ruins of a fishing station at Kambstún, which now form a grassy plot just below the mountain.

During the fishing season, people used to come here from the north, having crossed Vatnajökull to get to the sea. The easiest northern approach to the glacier is from the farm of Kálfafellsstadur, through the Stadardalur Valley, and this part of the glacier is known as the Heinabergsjökull. Although this is the easiest route it is still fairly dangerous and it must have been quite an exciting trip in the Middle Ages, and it must have been a dire necessity that forced the fishermen to make such a trip. Other people from the north would go to fish off Ingólfshöfdi, but they would come down from the glacier in the Morsárdalur Valley in Skaftafell National Park. When at the end of the sixteenth century, the climate throughout Iceland turned colder, but especially so in the glacier region, the annual migration south ended. Other sites to visit are the mountains of Papylisfjall, and

Höfn

especially the Klukkugil ravine, and the breathtaking scenery at Járnhus, near Gardhvammur.

On the Breidamerkur sands you can see some of the destruction wreaked by the glaciers over the last two or three hundred years. The river Jökulsá flows out into a large lagoon which is often host to huge icebergs, which break off from the glacier towering behind. In the east there is now a wasteland, which was woodland before it was destroyed by the advancing glacier. Fortunately, the history of this time is well recorded in the *Njálasaga*. In many ways history is still being created here by the constant geological activity.

The eastern shoreline of Iceland is very reminiscent of Norway with its deeply indented coastline and mountains which plunge steeply straight into the sea. The Icelandic word for these inlets is *vík*, and presumably this is where the word Vikings comes from.

The Eastern Fjords

The Eastern Fjords stretch from Berufjördur in the south which plunges north-westwards into the hinterland, to Borgarfjördur Eystri in the north. Between these two places there are many coastal villages to visit, although much of the population has moved away from the countryside, and most of the farms are now abandoned.

In the Eastern Fjords (Austfirdir in Icelandic), there is little sign of the volcanic activity that can be seen in most other parts of the country. This is because the land here is the oldest in Iceland and it consists mostly of basalt, which contains spar, pearlite, quartz and fossils. Crystals of spar, with their special property of double refraction — known as Iceland spar — have been recovered in the past for use in the optical industry, and there may be industrial possibilities for the pearlite as well.

Because many of the fjords are long and narrow, with towering sides, they are protected from the sea and make ideal shelters for vessels. In most of the inlets there is a fishing village, and the fishermen are some of the most skilled in the world. Not only do they have to contend with some of the most dangerous seas anywhere, their own coastline is littered with submerged rocks and reefs, which have caused many ships to founder.

Because the mountains inside the coast are so steep, travel used to be very difficult, but engineers solved the problem by building the roads wherever possible along the ridges of the hills, so that even though they are at high altitude, they do allow access.

There is no real coastal plain in this area because the mountains are so close to the sea, but behind the range is a plain, fertile enough for agriculture. Known as the **Fljótsdalshérad**, it reaches from a point just north of Austfirdir, and all the way south down the region, and encompasses some marvellous scenery. There are woods and lakes surrounded by lush vegetation and in the Fljótsdalshérad there are many farms. The region is dominated by the market town of Egilsstadir, which has an airfield and a good road network which makes it ideal as a base for touring. From here, the wild, eerie world of Iceland's interior can be explored; not far away is **Askja**, a volcano that has erupted many times in the last hundred years. It has a caldera up to 50sq km (20sq miles) in size in the Dyngjiufjöll mountains. A lake called Öskjuvatn was formed after the massive eruption in 1875, and it is the deepest in Iceland at 220m (722ft) deep and with an area of 12sq km (4.5sq miles). Beside the lake is the explosion crater Viti, formed on 29 March 1875; it is 100m (328ft) across, about 60m (200ft) deep and it is filled with water. Askja is a central volcano and it has erupted many times; 1961 was the last time. To reach the mountain a four-wheel drive vehicle is essential, and then a sturdy pair of walking boots. **Herdubreidarlindir** is an area of clear freshwater springs at the edge of the Ódádahraun, near the mountain of Herdubreid, often called the Queen of Iceland's Mountains. The area is lush and overgrown, and the springs were declared a nature reserve in 1974. This fertile region finally peters out in the south when it comes up against the northern edge of the Vatnajökull glacier.

The region can trace its history back to the earliest settlements of Iceland. Because it was the nearest coastline to Norway it was the first to be visited by the Norsemen in their explorations. They certainly landed here in the ninth century and some of them may have even come from the parts of Britain they had colonised. As in other parts of the south, there were Irish monks already living here in seclusion. The island off Berufjördur is called Papey, and is said to have derived its name from these Christians. It literally means Monks' Island.

There are even records that pirates from North Africa raided this coastline in the seventeenth century. Many records tell of the attacks by the 'Turks' on this coast and in other parts of south and east Iceland. Although the pickings cannot have been too rich, people were often taken away as slaves. There were two trading posts along this coast in the seventeenth and eighteenth centuries, at Rey-

Hornafjardarfljot, near Höfn

Jökuldalur near Haukstadir Farm

darfjördur and Djúpivogur. This was at the time of the strict Danish trading monopoly and it is only in the last 100 years or so that the region has really developed. Like much of Iceland's prosperity, the wealth came from the sea. Until the late nineteenth century, there were few people living in the region and the small population was isolated with little chance of mixing, because travel between settlements was so difficult. Then the Norwegians arrived, searching for good fishing ground, and they established many of the small coastal villages which still thrive today.

The villages were set up to handle the herring catches, and then whaling stations were established. The coastline is the nearest part of Iceland to Norway, and Norway's influence can still be seen in the architecture and names used by the people of Austfirdir. In 1918 when Iceland received its independence from Denmark, it banned all foreign fishing interests from operating from its territory, and the fortunes of the Eastern Fjords began to decline. Some of the people moved inland and tried to farm, but better sea travel and the need for fish restored the fortunes of the region.

New ports were established at Neskaupstadur, in Nordfjördur, which were much closer to the fishing grounds, and the region's economy boomed after World War II when the herring returned in massive shoals off the coast. By then, there had been considerable advances in fishing techniques, not only in catching, but also in handling and processing. It is still worth visiting one of the fjords in the summer, when the catches are being landed, to see the bustle and activity. The arrival of the trawlers is presaged by armies of birds calling loudly and swooping overhead. Then, it seems that every member of the community joins in to help with the work of unloading.

Again, this coastline is a must for naturalists, for it teems with birdlife and seals. Like other parts of the south and east coast, the seals are still hunted for their skins, and the fishermen and farmers see this as a valuable source of extra income.

The best way to see the true splendour of the Eastern Fjords is to visit them by boat, provided sufficient time is available, and there are a number that ply around the coast, calling briefly at the villages in the fjords. If time is more pressing, it is possible to fly to Egilsstadir from either Reykjavík or Akureyri and then hire a car, to drive in. There are many hotels, guesthouses, and campsites throughout the region, and the more time you have to spend exploring here the better.

There are a number of islands off the coast of the Eastern Fjords, the most famous of which are **Skrudur** in the Fáskrúdsfjördur and **Papey**. Both can be reached by ferry or local boat.

The eastern seashore has a very pleasant summer climate, and the landscape can be seen at its best during the summer months. **Búlandstindur**, which raises majestically to 1,069m (3,507ft), is thought by many to be the most beautiful summit in the east. It is best viewed from Djúpivogur or from the sea, but no matter from which direction you view it, it is magnificent.

Lagarfljót in Fljótsdalur is the second largest river in the east, running for about 140km (87 miles). The third largest lake in Iceland can be found in its upper reaches, and this 52sq km (20sq miles) wide stretch of water is said by legend to house the Lagarfljótsormur, a serpent-like creature, possibly Iceland's answer to the Loch Ness Monster. The lake is called **Lögurinn**.

Hallormsstadur, to the east of Lake Lögurinn, is the forest area which covers the site of an old manor house and church. The government decided to set up its experimental forestry centre here earlier this century. Scientists are trying to see which trees can cope best with the Icelandic climate and more than forty varieties from many countries have been planted. Varieties include mostly spruce and larch, but seeds and saplings have been brought in from the United States, Canada and Siberia.

Because of the forest, there is scenery here which is found almost nowhere else in Iceland, and because of this the area attracts many tourists. There is a very good camping ground at **Atlavík**, named after the pioneer settler Atli, on the shore of Lake Lögurinn. The river and lake are too cold to swim in, but there are many interesting walks in the area, and remember to look out for the 'monster'. There is a summer hotel. **Eidar** has a large district boarding school, which like most of the others in rural Iceland, is turned into a summer hotel during the 3-month-long vacation.

There are many tours of this area, and these can be arranged either locally or in Reykjavík. One of the best is a 5-hour tour which goes through the Hallormsstadur woods and round Lake Lögurinn and includes lunch. On the way it visits the Grímsá hydro-electric power station, the Valthjófsstadur church and the Skriduklaustur experimental farm.

The Valthjófsstadur church is famous for its carved wooden door which dates back to the turn of the twelfth century, although only a replica is to be seen, as the original is now preserved in the National

Museum in Reykjavík. The experimental farm used to be the site of a fifteenth-century monastery, and some ruins of this can still be seen. It was here in the eighteenth century that the first reindeer were introduced into the country from Scandinavia by Hans Wium, the local sheriff. The reindeer still roam wild in the highlands of eastern Iceland and occasionally they are shot and their meat offered in local restaurants — and it is delicious. The present buildings, designed by a German just before the outbreak of World War II, were the home of the famous Icelandic author Gunnar Gunnarsson, who donated them to the state. Part of them have been converted into a local folk museum.

Nearby is the country's third largest waterfall **Hengifoss**, and also on this tour you can see the remains of a stone-free church, and Mjóanes, the place where the warrior poet Helgi Arinbjörnsson lived many centuries ago.

While in the area the waterfall at **Lagarfoss** and the seal colony at **Húsey** should be visited. A stay in this region should also include a trip into the interior or on the Vatnajökull. There are many such tours organised and local guides to escort travellers. The best way in is either on horseback, or in a four-wheel drive vehicle.

The area is also good for bird watchers, and fly fishermen, and there is some excellent trout fishing to be had here. A licence is needed but it is not expensive.

Egilsstadir is a town that has mushroomed in the last two decades from a small market centre into a flourishing community with a lot of accommodation provided by a hotel, guest houses, sleeping bag accommodation and on farms nearby. There is a hospital, a number of restaurants and cafés, and a tourist information centre and travel bureau. Fishing permits can be obtained here, there is horse riding available, as well as a swimming pool and museum. It is also the site of the largest airport in the east, and is a natural touring centre, because from here you can travel in any direction. The town lies beside Lake Lögurinn and is at the main junction of the roads from Reykjavík and Akureyri with routes from them to all the fjords. There is a magnificent view of the whole area and the snow-capped peaks in the background, from the Seydisfjördur road just above Egilsstadir.

There is much to see and do, especially for those interested in nature or walking. It is possible to walk down into the Eyvindará ravine and also to visit **Gálgaklettur**, a small town where there is a stone marking the scene of the last execution in this district. In the

Seydisfjördur

Eskifjördur

eighteenth century, a man called Valtyr was put to death. The reason for his execution has been obscured by time, but local legend has it that he was innocent of any crime.

Seydisfjördur is a town standing on the fjord of the same name and for many years it was the largest town on the east coast. It is still the ferry port for ships arriving from the Faroes and the drive over the mountains to Egilsstadir is one of the most spectacular in Iceland, if not a little daunting if it is your first experience of driving in the country. As you climb away from the town, the valley is surrounded by sheer cliffs and scores of plunging waterfalls. The mountains rise to 1,028m (3,371ft) and avalanches and rock slides are not uncommon. After climbing past the river which plunges in a series of spectacular falls, the road crosses a stark plateau with Heidarvatn on your right, a large, gaunt lake at 585m (1,918ft). It can be very cold and windy up here, but as you pass the lake you soon start your descent and can see Egilsstadir deep in the valley below.

Seydisfjördur is still a charming town, and the prettiest along the east coast. It began as a trading post in 1834 but it prospered in the latter part of the century. The town still has many wooden houses dating from the turn of the century, showing the strong Norwegian influences in the area. The decline of recent years has now been halted and there is a hotel, youth hostel, community centre, cinema and a campsite nearby at Fjardarsel. **Reydarfjördur** also started life as a trading post although its real name is Búdareyri. It grew in size with the completion of the highway in 1909, and during World War II was the home of one of the Allied Forces' largest bases. It is another useful place to stop and from which to explore the surrounding countryside. It has two hotels and a campsite, as well as all the usual facilities. Although industry is becoming important, the town's economy is still based on fishing. A coastal steamer calls here.

Iceland's highest road suitable for motor vehicles travels through this area linking Eskifjördur and Nordfjördur using the Oddsskard Pass. In places the road is 660m, or more than 2,160ft above sea level.

Eskifjördur is another town named after the fjord on which it stands. The fjord is about 2km ($1\frac{1}{4}$ miles) long and up to 6km ($3\frac{3}{4}$ miles) wide. Much of the surrounding area is protected because of its outstanding natural beauty and the wealth of natural history to be found there. The protected area is known as the Hólmanes, and this is the area between Eskifjördur and Reydarfjördur. The most easterly point in Iceland, the **Gerpir Headland** can also be visited.

From Cape Hólmanes rises the 985m (3,232ft) high peak of Hólmatindur. Although it looks beautiful behind the town it is so high and so close it actually wipes out the daylight. Between the end of September until April it is very unusual to see the sun, which is masked behind the mountain. Fishing is the mainstay of the town and most of the other industries are associated with this, including a freezer plant. Dried fish is also produced and is very useful for campers or backpackers going into the interior. In the same way that American cowboys chewed strips of dried beef or jerky on the trail, the Icelanders chew dried fish. The fish has a number of advantages for backpackers; it is light, convenient, does not need heating and supplies plenty of nourishment. Although at first, when a piece is bitten off, it tastes just like a strip of wood, it gradually becomes softer, tastes fishier, and it is very enjoyable. The action also stimulates the salivary glands so it can be useful to bite a piece if you are feeling particularly dry. At Eskifjördur there is a hotel, a number of restaurants and all the services; there is also an interesting museum which has a ship's mast and rigging outside. It is open from 2-5pm from June to September. There is also a very moving memorial to fishermen lost at sea. There is a well signposted campsite, swimming pool, filling station, garage and café.

It is worth the detour north to Neskaupstadur on Route 92. The road takes you through the Oddsskard Pass (at 632m, 2,072ft), the highest in Iceland) and through an eerie 600m long (1,968ft) tunnel guarded by massive pivoted metal gates. It is narrow and not too well lit and a lot of water seems to drip down from the roof, but there are spectacular views both just before and just after you pass through the tunnel. Snow lies in pockets all year round along the pass.

Neskaupstadur nestles on the left-hand side of Nordfjördur with the mountain finger of Bardsnes jutting out into the sea to the right giving the harbour a lot of protection. As you descend down the mountain, the valley opens up before you with its farms and fertile fields. Neskaupstadur is now the largest town in the east, again with fishing as the backbone of its economy, although there is some agriculture carried on inland. The town has a swimming pool and a community centre where you can get food and lodging. There is also a campsite and hotel, swimming pool, shops, restaurant, hospital and natural history museum.

Fáskrúdsfjördur was established towards the end of the nine-

Valley above Seydisfjördur

teenth century and became the main base for French fishermen operating in and around the Eastern Fjords. The French built their own hospital and chapel here but no trace of these buildings now remains, although there is the French seamen's graveyard. There is now no trace of the French because they left when the era of the sailing boats ended at the beginning of this century. The town is still charming with many different coloured houses, pretty gardens and lots of greenery. While fishing is the main occupation in the town, the hardships of farming can easily be seen by the number of deserted farms throughout the Eastern Fjords.

Stödvarfjördur stands on the fjord which gives it its name, and is another of the bustling little fishing villages to be found all along this coast. There is a freezer plant which provides most of the area's employment. There is also a car repair shop, bank, store, and infirmary.

Breiddalsvík stands by the cove bearing the same name and has only existed for a short time. It grew up a few decades ago when the fishing improved off the eastern coast and most of the inhabitants are now employed in the fishing industry. It has a new hotel and there is a small area of grass behind the hotel where you can camp for a small fee. The hotel is being extended and has a restaurant, and the small campsite has two small cabins, each containing washing facilities, water and toilet. There is a Hotel Edda at Stadaborg, about 7km (4 miles) west of the town.

The road out of Breiddalsvík heading for Stödvarfjördur, is spectacular with plunging cliffs on one side, and towering mountains with cascading waterfalls on the other. Great care is needed when driving, especially in wet weather when the pot holes fill with water and you cannot be sure how deep they are.

5

THE WEST COAST
AND WESTERN FJORDS

T he western coast really comprises the districts of Borgarfjördur,
Snaefellsnes, and Dalir. In this region can be found almost every
type of geological formation and it is extremely attractive to bird
watchers.

Off the **Borgarfjördur Bay**, there is a lowland plain whose fingers
reach between the mountains in a series of valleys. Here you will find
fast running rivers and some of the best salmon fishing Iceland has
to offer. Hvalfjördur is a long narrow bay and is the home for the only
land-based whaling station in Iceland, although as mentioned earlier,
its future is uncertain now that the country has agreed to curtail
whaling operations. There is also an iron ore refinery to be found
here.

Borgarnes is one of the few coastal towns which does not rely on
fishing for its economy. It is the commercial and trading centre for the
region and has a hotel, sports stadium, golf course, and swimming
pool. The campsite is beside the road leading into the town. There is
now a new bridge just outside Borgarnes which crosses Borgarfjördur and greatly reduces the journey to Reykjavík and the
south. This district is one of the most fertile agricultural regions in
Iceland with many large farms and ranches. There is also a park in
the town where Skallagrímur, the original settler of the district, is said

153

to be buried. With his son Egil, a famous Viking and poet, he is supposed to have farmed at Borg, a few minutes' drive from the town, but nothing remains of this today.

Snaefellsnes is a long mountainous peninsula separating the two largest bays in Iceland, Faxaflói and Breidafjördur which means 'Broad Firth'. A road follows the line of the bay and another runs out into the peninsula. The area is predominantly occupied with fishing and farming, although other industries are now taking a more important role. The area is dominated by Snaefellsjökull, an extinct volcano on the tip of the Snaefellsnes peninsula, which can even be seen from Reykjavík on fine days. The long since dead volcano is now tipped with a glacier.

The mountains in the area are mainly of basalt although they contain many other interesting minerals such as rhyolite, tuff and breccia. There are many lakes, and the rivers tend to be short because of the mountainous nature of the countryside. There are a number of routes across the mountains to allow the traveller to journey from south to north, and the best crossing points are at Fródárheidi (361m, 1,184ft), and Kerlingarskard (311m, 1,020ft).

Between Búdir and Ólafsvík, towards the western tip of the peninsula, the promontory is less than 20km (12$^1/_2$ miles) wide, but it increases in breadth towards the east. In the east of the region, to the south of the central ridge of mountains, there is a grassy plain which accommodates most of the agriculture. The scenery here is varied, and there are marshes, with many interesting birds, as well as sandy beaches, lagoons and numerous small lakes.

The northern shore has little lowland, as the mountains plunge straight into the sea, and the coastline is deeply indented with fjords, such as Álftafjördur, Kolgrafafjördur and Grundarfjördur. The fjords, with their deep water, and protected by the towering mountains, make ideal anchorages and many ports and fishing villages have been established here.

There are extensive lavafields at the foot of the glacier, at Búdahraun, Drangahraun, and Neshraun, which were formed when lava flowed from Snaefellsjökull crater and others in the area long before Iceland was first settled. In many places the lava runs straight into the sea and produces a weird and wonderful landscape of strange twisted shapes, towering lava cliffs, pillars and so on. There are lighthouses at Malarrif and Öndverdarnes and another lavafield at Berserkjahraun, which flowed from craters near Bjarnarhöfn on the

Búdardalur

north coast. Carbon dioxide springs can be found in many places on Snaefellsnes, caused by the turbulent volcanic activity. The early settlers nicknamed the springs 'beer wells' because the water with its sparkle was so good to drink. It can still be drunk today and is said to be good for the health.

On the north coast of Snaefellsnes and to the east of Stykkishólmur is a low-lying, wooded shore leading to the Dalir, a region of hills, grassy valleys and clear rivers. Further up the coast to the north, there is a trading centre at **Búdardalur**, nestling in the shadow of another mountainous peninsula jutting out into the sea. At the tip of this peninsula reaching out into Breidafjördur, there are many small islands, said to be so numerous that they have never been counted. In places there are so many small islands that the sea is forced through narrow gaps, increasing its speed and creating tricky currents which make all navigation in this area dangerous.

Most of the islands are low and have grassy vegetation, although the Klakkeyjar group have strange pyramid shaped hills which can be spotted many miles away. The biggest island off the coastline is Brokey. In the past most of the islands were inhabited by farmers, but now almost all are abandoned except for Flatey in the centre of Breidafjördur, although summer cottages have been built on others for occasional use.

The western coastline has a rich history, clearly chronicled in many of the Sagas. It was the first part of the country to be seriously settled by the Norsemen in the ninth and tenth centuries, and there are vivid records of these early days in the *Eyrbyggja*, *Laxdaela* and *Sturlunga* Sagas, written in the thirteenth century.

Many of the settlers to these parts came via the Hebrides or Ireland, especially those who made their homes on and around Snaefellsnes. Here, there are still strong traces of their Celtic origin, and recent medical tests have proved that the Icelanders are more closely related to the Celts than they are to the Scandinavians.

The method of creation of the Sagas is not known, although people everywhere have tried to record their early history in similar ways. Most literate people of this time can be traced to the monasteries, and it is thought the Celts played a great part in the writing of the Sagas. Today, there are still many place names which have Celtic links and many start with the Icelandic name for Irish. There is Írafell (Irish mountain), Íraklettur (Irish rock), Írskaleid (Irish route) and Írskutóftir (Irish homes)

British vessels, which traded off this western coast in the fifteenth century, are also believed to have been responsible for places being given such names as Bretahraun, Bretalaekur and Kumbaravogur although the names are probably earlier. The word 'Snaefell' of course, is of Scandinavian origin, and is also the name for the mountain on the Isle of Man, which was once itself a Viking colony.

The first settler to this coastline is thought to have been Thórólfur Mostraskegg, who arrived from Norway in 884. He landed near Stykkishólmur and named the promontory there Thórsnes, because it was where the pillars from his Thor temple were washed ashore. It was customary for the Norsemen to choose their home by casting overboard a sacred or treasured possession. If it drifted ashore they reasoned that the gods were happy and had chosen this as the site for settlement. Reykjavík was chosen in the same way, although legend has it that it took Arnarson several months to discover just where his 'sacrifices' had been washed up.

Mostraskegg established the first parliament in Iceland. The 'thing' or legislative assembly met on Thórsnes many times before the National Assembly was founded at Thingvellir to the east of

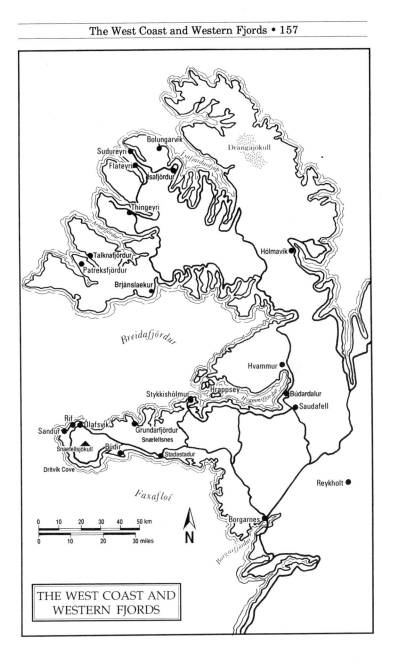

THE WEST COAST AND
WESTERN FJORDS

Reykjavík in 930.

There were many other famous settlers in this area, according to the Sagas, including Audur the Deepminded, the widow of a Viking king of Dublin. She had adopted the Christian faith and had travelled to Iceland via the Hebrides.

The coastline has had a stormy history and it often resisted dictates from Denmark. British traders often plied here without the necessary permission from Denmark and in 1457, the local officials became so annoyed that they tried to stop trade. The British simply killed the governor and things continued without further interference. After the British, there was a long tradition of trading with the Germans but international trade with any other country than Denmark almost came to an end with the introduction of the Danish trading monopoly in the early seventeenth century.

There are many interesting things to see in this area including the glacier **Snaefellsjökull**, which is now one of the smallest ice caps in Iceland having an area of only about 11 sq km (4 sq miles). The glacier has a number of peaks, the highest of which is 1,446m (4,744ft), in the far north-west of the peninsula. It is possible to climb to the top, but late spring and early summer are the best times, as it can be dangerous later in the summer when crevasses appear in the ice. The peak was first climbed by two Icelanders in 1753, and then by an English team of climbers in 1789. The French author, Jules Verne, used the crater at Snaefellsjökull as the entry point in his story *Journey to the Centre of the Earth*.

The best starting point for the climb is near Arnarstapi on the southern slopes, and here the path is relatively easy to climb and easy to follow. The climb will take about 4 hours although guides are available and it is best to be accompanied by one of them, if you are not an experienced climber. There is a mountain hut on this southern side maintained by the Iceland Tourist Association.

The area is easily accessible from Reykjavík and there is a regular bus service into the region, and many organised tours, which can last anything from a few hours to several days. Naturalists will find much of interest here. There are hotels at Stykkishólmur on the north coast of Snaefellsnes and Búdir in the south, as well as guesthouses at Ólafsvík and Grundarfjördur. Equally, it is possible to pitch a tent almost anywhere.

The southern shore of Snaefellsnes, between the salmon rivers of Hítará and Haffjardará in the east, is dominated by the **Eldbor-**

Arnarstapi with the Snæfells glacier in the background

garhraun lavafield. It is possible to walk for about 30 minutes from the main road to the Eldborg crater which was the site of a major eruption. Near the farm of Raudimelur, west of Haffjardará, the waters from the carbon dioxide springs, or the 'beer wells' can be sampled. The largest such springs on Snaefellsnes are to be found here. Around here there are also spectacular basalt columns.

In 1936 a French exploration ship, the *Pourquoi Pas?*, was lost here with nearly all hands, near the mouth of the river Straumfjardará, which is also famous for its salmon fishing. About half-way between here and Búdir is the parsonage of Stadastadur, where the historian Ari the Wise lived in the early twelfth century and where he wrote the *Íslendingabók*, which chronicled the early history of the country.

There are a number of other carbon dioxide springs around **Búdir**, together with a farm, Ölkelda, named after one. In Búdir there is a swimming pool built by a farmer but open to the public which utilises a hot spring. Búdir was once an important port, but is now only a hamlet with a summer hotel. It is a useful base for exploring the Búdaklettur crater and the lava, in which can be found many rare species of ferns and wild flowers.

Also to be seen near here are the cliffs and caves at the fishing village of Arnarstapi and Hellnar, the Stapafell mountain, famous for its echoing caves, and the impressive towering Hraundrangar rocks near the lighthouse at Malarrif. At the western end of Snaefellsnes is **Dritvik Cove**, which although some kilometres off the main road, is worth a visit. There are the remnants of an ancient fishing village, where the people would venture far out to sea in open rowing boats. The northern coast of Snaefellsnes is uninhabited until you arrive at Hellissandur, also called **Sandur**, which is another fishing village. It is the westernmost village of Snaefellsnes and although there is some agriculture inland, the population level has stayed virtually unchanged all this century.

There is also the fishing port of **Rif**, with its new harbour, which is now one of the busiest villages along the coast. It is not to be confused with **Ólafsvík**, farther to the east, another fishing village whose population has grown rapidly in recent years, where there is now a hotel, restaurant and community centre. A storage house built in 1841 can still be seen and is thought to be the only building of its kind left in Iceland. The building has now been converted into a small craft museum showing how the people worked a century ago, and the sorts of tools they used. Ólafsvík is Iceland's oldest trading centre,

PLACES OF INTEREST
IN THE WESTERN FJORDS

Ísafjördur
Local ferry-boat tours of the
coast from here; sailings tie in
with air service to Reykjavík.
Also local folk museum, art
gallery, etc.
Very good skiing in winter with
nearby ski lodge.

Langeyri
Old whaling station which can be
visited.

Látrabjarg
The most westerly point in
Europe; spectacular scenery and
innumerable birds.

gaining its authorisation from King Christian V of Denmark on 26
March 1687. Vessels regularly plied to Denmark, Britain and as far
afield as Spain. *The Swan* is the port's most famous vessel and it
traded out of Ólafsvík for 116 years until it was damaged beyond
repair in an accident which beached her on the approaches to the port
in 1893, the longest ever in the world.

Although Ólafsvík only had a population of 92 in 1801, this had
grown to 255 in 1890 and 612 by 1901, making it the seventh largest
urban area in Iceland. It now has about 1,200 inhabitants. The
campsite is just outside the village, and there is a golf course and
swimming pool. There is a very attractive modern architecture church
consecrated in 1967 which stands on a small hill close to the town,
believed to be the site of the farm of the settler Olafur Belgur.

Snaefellsjökull dominates the land behind the town, and many
people believe this is the most beautiful glacier in Iceland. On a good
day it can even be spotted from Reykjavík. There are many good
walks in and around the glacier and there is a good road leading
towards it.

The northern shore of Snaefellsnes is rugged and mountainous,
characterised by steep cliffs and fjords with many fishing villages,
nestling on the rocky inlets.

Grundarfjördur is a fishing village with a growing population,
completely trapped by mountains and the sea. It has a hotel and is
a good base for visiting one of the country's most beautiful mountains, Kirkjufell, which climbs to 463m (1,519ft). The campsite is at
Kverná, about 1km (half a mile) from the village.

Lóndrangar rocks, south of Ólafsvík

At Hraunfjördur the lavafield disappears into the sea. **Stykkishólmur** is the largest town on Snaefellsnes, and fishing provides the main occupation. The area also has an agricultural hinterland, so many industries connected with this can be found in the town. There is a hotel and guesthouse, restaurant, filling stations, swimming pool, tourist information centre and bus station. The campsite is by the sports field. There is an airstrip and the area around the town is very beautiful. Helgafell, a small mountain which raises to 73m (240ft) above the sea is the subject of many folk stories and legends. It is said, for example, that if someone walks up to the top for the first time, without looking back or speaking a single word, they will be allowed three wishes on reaching the top, provided they are not bad wishes, and the person making them faces the east.

The mountain is also said to have been the home of Gudrún, heroine of the *Laxdaela* Saga, and the abode of Ari the Wise, and the chieftain Snorri Godi. It was also the site of a twelfth-century Augustinian monastery which lasted for 400 years. The island's first assembly met at Thingvellir a few miles away, which is not to be confused with the site of the National Assembly to the east of Reykjavík. Nearby is the spectacular Drápuhlídar mountain, famous for its varied colours caused by the presence of rhyolite, jasper and pyrites.

At **Bólstadur** in Álftafjördur you can see the remains of a tenth-century farm which was excavated in the 1920s, and the whole of this district featured heavily in the *Eyrbyggja* Saga. To the east there is the parsonage at Breidabólstadur and the Drangar rocks, where Eirík the Red committed the murders which led to him being outlawed. He fled to Greenland, which is how the island to the west of Iceland came to be settled. It was on the islands of Klakkeyjar, just off the coast, that he prepared for his expedition.

On Hrappsey, now owned by Iceland University, the island's first magazine was printed in the years 1773-95.

The eastern shore of Hvammsfjördur, known as **Dalasysla**, is also rich in historical legend and again featured heavily in the Sagas. The home of Eirík the Red is at the farm at Stóra Vatnshorn, and his son Leif Eiríksson, the discoverer of North America in 1000, is said to have been born at Eiríksstadir. Hjardarholt, at the mouth of Laxárdalur, was the birthplace of Kjartan, hero of the *Laxdaela* Saga, and Höskuldsstadir was the home of Höskuldur who was married to the Irish princess Melkorka, and was father of Ólafur the Peacock.

The only trading and service centre in the Dalasysla district is Búrdar-
dalur, which has a hotel, tourist shop, community centre and restaurant.

To the south is **Saudafell**, the home of a thirteenth-century
chieftain who went on a pilgrimage to Rome. It was in this region that
the clan feuds took place in the twelfth and thirteenth centuries which
eventually led to Iceland losing its independence to Norway in 1262.
It was at Saudafell also that the last Catholic bishop, Jón Arason, and
his two sons were captured, and then taken to Skálholt and beheaded
in 1550.

The farm at **Hvammur** was the home of Audur the Deepminded
and the birthplace of the Sturlunga Clan in about 1115. On the cliffs
at Krosshólaborg, there is a stone cross marking the spot where
Audur used to pray.

The northern coast of Dalasysla, Skardsströnd, gets its name
from Skard, a farm which has been in the hands of the same family
since the eleventh century. In the fifteenth century it was the home of
the local governor Björn Thorleifsson, whose wife Ólöf the Rich
avenged his murder by the British at Rif by killing some British
fishermen and forcing others to work as slaves on the farm. The new
church contains an altar-piece dating back to the fifteenth century,
donated by Ólöf.

Other places of interest in the west include Reykholt, which was
once the home of Snorri Sturluson, one of Iceland's best known
scholars and author of *Heimskringla, Snorri Edda* and other works.
There is a pool here which he is believed to have used and a tunnel
between the pool and Snorri's house has been partially rebuilt. A
boarding school is used as a summer hotel. Nearby Húsafell is a large
forest of birch trees and the location for many important outdoor
events. There are three large craters with strange, eerie shapes just
off the road in Borgarfjördur called Grábrók. There is a restaurant
here.

North of Svínaskard, Kastalinn, a rock formation resembling a
fortress, can be seen, which offers one of the best vantage points in
the area.

The Western Fjords

The Western Fjords (Vestfirdir) form the most westerly part of
Iceland, and geologically are very old. The mountains are high and
the coastline indented by deep narrow fjords. There are many fishing

Stykkishólmur Harbour

villages along the coast and fishing and fish processing forms the major source of employment.

The most westerly point is **Látrabjarg**, which is a cliff teeming with birdlife during the summer months. This cliff is, in fact, the most westerly point in Europe and is only 278km (173 miles) from Greenland. There is spectacular scenery here in the mountains and moorland.

The whole of the Western Fjords area sticks out into the sea and the width of land connecting it to the mainland is so narrow, less than 16km (10 miles) wide, that it looks as if it might snap off at any time.

The region is one of basalt cliffs towering in places to 400m (1,312ft) high while the highest peak, Kaldabakur, is just under 1,000m high (a little over 3,000ft). The two largest fjords on the north coast are **Arnarfjördur** and **Ísafjardardjúp** and both have several smaller fjords running from them. All the fjords on this western coast tend to run from north-west to south-east. The east coast of the peninsula is known as Strandir, and the extreme north is called Hornstrandir, which gets its name from the word '*horn*' meaning cape. It is the most northerly point of Iceland.

Because this is the oldest geological area of Iceland there has been no volcanic activity here for many years and there is little lava in evidence. There is an area of hot springs near Reykjanes at the south-eastern end of Ísafjardardjúp. Because of the steepness of the slopes, there is little vegetation, and the small amount visible is confined to the narrow coastal strips of the fjords.

There is a small glacier, Drangajökull, at 925m (3,035ft) in the north-east, but another one, Gláma, has now disappeared because of the increasing warmth of the climate. The glacier started to disappear in about 1600 and had completely disappeared by 1900.

In many ways this area has a history that closely resembles that of the Scottish Highlands. There were many powerful chieftains in this area from the thirteenth to sixteenth centuries, and their families were often feuding. The history of this period can be read in the Sagas of *Gísli*, *Hávardur* and *Fóstbroedur*, all of which are concerned with the Vestfirdir.

It was in this region that Jón Sigurdsson was born in 1811. He was later to become the champion of Iceland's independence movement.

Again, as with the whole western coast, there are many names here to recall the Celtic influence on the region. There is Patreksfjördur, in the southern part of the Western Fjords, which was named after Bishop Patrick from the Hebrides. There is also Brjáns-laekur, which means Brian's Brook, and other Irish-derived names.

This part of the country has often played host to foreigners. In the past, the ports and trading centres were often visited by German and British traders, and more recently fishermen from several nations have used the harbours to shelter from the severe storms that sweep the area. Although there are still rich fishing grounds off the west coast of Iceland and in the Denmark Strait between Greenland and Iceland, the new fishing limits now exclude most foreign vessels, and the British deep sea fleet is so reduced that its vessels look for catches nearer to home.

Because the district is so close to the Arctic, its climate is somewhat colder than the rest of Iceland, but in the summer it can still be quite warm in the shelter of the fjords, and there is the additional bonus of many weeks of perpetual daylight which allows exploration of the countryside at leisure.

Although the idea of the continual daylight for several weeks seems strange to us, it is something which is easy to become accustomed to and can quickly be taken advantage of. For climbers and walkers there is no longer such urgency, late in the day, to look for a suitable campsite. If tiredness sets in, it is easy simply to stop, cook a meal and then sleep for 2 or 3 hours at a time when necessary. It is a very secure feeling to know that if you are driving over a mountain road, the sun is not suddenly going to set, leaving you literally in the dark, and this corner of Iceland, because of its position, tends to have longer periods of permanent daylight than the rest of the country.

For a naturalist it is interesting to see how the birds adapt to these conditions. There is no longer the frantic feeding rush that birds further south have to follow in order to keep their nestlings satisfied from dawn to dusk. Here in this mountainous corner you may see the magnificent white tailed eagle. There are a few pairs still breeding here, but there are no clear signs of just how endangered the species is. In the summer there are thousands of nesting birds all along the coast, especially puffins, arctic tern and eider.

Sheepfarming is now the major form of agriculture and most other forms of cultivation have ceased, with many of the farms in the north now abandoned. Many of the people have moved to the fishing villages where processing industries have sprung up to handle the rich catches available off the coast. In times gone by there were a

Boats moored near Brjánslaekur

The flower garden in Ísafjördur

number of whaling stations along this coastline, set up by the Norwegians at Flateyri, Hesteyri and Tálknafjördur. The centre for the country's shark fishing industry was also here. Neither of these occupations are now pursued here.

The best base for touring the area is **Ísafjördur**, the principal town and main trading centre for the region. It is on Skutulsfjördur, surrounded by mountains on three sides and the sea on the other. It has been the capital of the Western Fjords for at least 200 years, since the King of Denmark lifted Iceland's trade monopoly. Then it was chosen to be one of six commercial and industrial centres in Iceland. A few houses dating from the eighteenth and nineteenth centuries can still be seen. The town is still predominantly a fishing centre, especially for shrimps, and it has an excellent natural harbour. There are, however, many other industries in and around the town including a flourishing boatworks. There is an airstrip with daily flights to Reykjavík as well as trips to other airfields in the area such as Thingeyri, Flateyri and Patreksfjördur. The town has hotels, restaurants, a folk museum, swimming pool, tourist information centre and campsite in Tungudalur, 4km ($2\frac{1}{2}$ miles) from the town, although there is a bus link. There is also a hospital, community centre and cinema. The town makes a good base for summer walking trips, or winter skiing, and there are a number of popular boat trips to Hornstrandir and Jökulfirdir.

Because of the mountainous nature of the countryside, travel used to be very difficult, and was almost impossible during the winter months. Now, the building of airstrips at Ísafjördur and a number of other villages has overcome many of these problems.

The area is also popular in the winter with skiers, and there is a ski lodge a short distance from Ísafjördur (about 3km, 1.8 miles) which is open from February until May, depending on the snow. The lodge is at an altitude of 200m (656ft) and has both rooms and dormitories for people with their own sleeping bags. The best skiing is to be had between March and April and there are some very good runs. The lodge is open during the summer as a base for hikers and climbers.

There are many organised tours from Ísafjördur which can be arranged locally or in Reykjavík. If you have time, certainly the best way of seeing the spectacular countryside is by boat. There is a daily tour in the summer from Ísafjördur on the local ferry boat which takes several hours and visits all the interesting places on route, including the islands of Aedaey and Vigur. Food is served on board, and it is possible to take this day trip from Reykjavík because the scheduled air services have been worked out to coincide with it. It is a long day, but well worth it if time is limited. If more time is available, a much more rewarding visit is achieved by staying for a day or two.

There are taxis which are willing to take passengers to other points of interest, and if the taxi is shared, there is no reason why it should be an expensive outing. Equally, there are bus services to places such as Thingeyri, but check the timetable because they do not always run every day, and it could be a long way to walk back.

It is possible to travel by ferry from Ísafjördur across the fjord to Kaldalón and then to the Drangajökull glacier which reaches almost to the sea. During the summer, there are regular Sunday sailings around the uninhabited islands and remote fjords in northern Ísafjördur. The next fjord, Álftafjördur, can also be reached, either by car or by a limited bus service. Here there are some magnificent views and one can visit the old whaling station at Langeyri.

The northern tip of the Western Fjords is desolate and uninhabited, and access to it is difficult, but it is the perfect place for a backpacking trip provided everything necessary for the trip is carried in the pack. There are no facilities at all, no shops and no medical treatment. So, if a trip in this area is planned, it is essential to go with someone experienced, and preferably as part of a large group; and please tell someone in advance where you are going, and how long you expect to be away. This is one of Iceland's most unexplored regions and very few tourists brave a trip here, which is a pity because it is an unspoilt, beautiful countryside where it is possible to get away from it all. It is possible to take a boat from Ísafjördur on a sightseeing trip along the coast.

Vatnsfjördur, due south, is most famous for being the place where the country received its name. It was here that Flóki Valgerdarson saw ice-floes drifting on the sea, and gave the country the name Iceland. It could have been given a very different name had he landed in the summer, because the fertile land surrounding the valley is lush with green vegetation, and the fjord has one of the warmest climates in Iceland.

Patreksfjördur, is the town on the fjord of the same name; most of its people are engaged in fishing or associated industries. There is a hospital, community centre, restaurant and cinema. There is also an airfield with regular flights to Reykjavík. **Talknafjördur** is another fishing village named after the fjord on which it stands. **Bíldudalur** is a prosperous fishing village on the southern side of Arnafjördur. Many of the country's finest shrimps are caught in the fjord and there is a processing plant in the town.

The oldest trading centre in the area is **Thingeyri**, which has a hotel, open all year. **Flateyri** is a town by Önundarfjördur which relies on fishing and agriculture for its livelihood.

Sudureyri is a fishing port which can be reached by driving over the 518m (1,700ft) high Botnsheidi Pass. Coastal vessels regularly stop here, and there is an airstrip, cinema, community centre and restaurant.

One of the oldest yet still active fishing ports in the country is **Bolungarvík**. The first motor-driven fishing boats in Iceland were operated from this port. The town has a hotel, airstrip, infirmary, community centre and heated swimming pool. **Hólmavík** is a fishing village which became a trading centre towards the end of the last century. It is now also the centre for the flourishing agricultural hinterland. It has an infirmary and hotel.

View from Gufufjördur

Driving along the West Coast and the Western Fjords

Although most of the roads in the region are made from gravel, it is possible to cover quite long distances in comparatively short spaces of time. Hopefully, if you are driving the ring road anti-clockwise, you should have enough confidence by now to drive at the fastest possible safe speed along these roads. There are stretches of quite stunning scenery, however, and many places which are worth stopping for, either to explore or photograph.

As with many other roads through Iceland you will see cairns, or piles of stones beside the road. These date back to the times when there were no roads, and these cairns were the only indication the traveller had that he was still heading in the right direction. In this region, the farms are 25km (15 or so miles) or more apart, and a century or so ago that must have been a daunting journey in bad weather.

If you are coming across from Akureyri, it is a good idea to leave the ring road and take Route 59 across Laxardalsheidi, a rocky and imposing landscape to Búdardalur. In Búdardalur you can drive down

Waterfall in the Western Fjords

to the beach and the smell of seaweed is very strong here. After the town you then have a choice of routes. You can either head south on Route 60 through the mountains to link up with the ring road at Dalsmynni, and then down to Borgarnes, or you can take Route 57 and head west to explore Snaefellsnes peninsula and the settlements along its north coast.

There are a lot of ranches in the area and horses on the road can be a hazard, so be on the alert for them. It is quite a common sight to see a string of horses being driven by a team of riders along the road, and it is safest to pull in and let them pass. If they are in ahead of you, they will usually pull off the road at a suitable point and let you pass — but do so slowly.

Route 57 follows the southern shore of Hvammsfjördur, and the grass soon gives way to rocks and mosses. The rivers have carved mini-canyons in the rocks as they have forced their way to the sea. You have to take Route 58 to divert off to Stykkishólmur, but it is worth the visit. There is a new church being built and a very good baker's shop. Then, you have the choice again of continuing westwards or cutting across the peninsula and heading south.

The road west, on Route 57 takes you to Grundarfjördur, Ólafsvík, Rif and Hellissandur before it turns south following the headland round. The road changes its number several times as you drive east along the southern shores of the peninsula — first the 574, then the 572, and finally the 54 which will take you back to Borgarnes.

The road round the peninsula is passable in either a two- or four-wheel drive vehicle but great care should be exercised when taking roads through the mountains. There are two such routes — 54 and 56 — and these can be very muddy, wet and slippery if there has been rain. Snow lies in pockets in the mountains right through the year.

Because of the damage caused to the roads by the winter weather it is not uncommon to suddenly come across a works gang with bulldozers and cranes filling in holes in the road and reinforcing the sides of the road. Often, the only thing you can do is switch off the car engine and enjoy the view until it is safe to go on and you are waved through.

The new bridge at Borgarnes has cut many miles off the trip to Reykjavík, and the road improves considerably, most of it being metalled.

There are hundreds of horses kept on ranches here, and the farms follow the coast all the way down to Reykjavík, hugging the shores and dominated by Esja (914m, 2,997ft) whose slopes roll down to the narrow coastal plain.

As you round the headland at Saurbaer, with its Lutheran church, you catch your first glimpse of Reykjavík in the distance across the waters. The church is dedicated to Hallgrímur Pétersson, one of Iceland's finest poets, who was pastor to the parish 300 years ago and who died of leprosy, once rife on the island. He wrote many hymns and his greatest work *Passíusálmar*, a glorification of the Passion of Christ, has been translated into more languages than any other Icelandic work.

It is a fascinating journey. You have horses, cattle and sheep for company beside the road, and thousands of ducks, especially the splendid eider, hugging the coastline. Things worth stopping for along the way are the whaling stations at Hvítanes (and the oil tanks, a permanent eye-sore and reminder of World War II) and Borgarnes, and Glymur, at 200m (656ft) high, the country's highest waterfall.

6

THE NORTH
OF ICELAND

The north of Iceland is a lush farming area with broad valleys and some of the best rivers for salmon fishing. Transport around the area is relatively easy as there are good roads and some airstrips. There are many fishing villages along this stretch of coastline.

There are also many places to visit if you are interested in wildlife; of special note are the two islands of Málmey and Drangey which have interesting bird populations.

The northern and north-eastern regions contain some of the jewels of Iceland's rich treasure chest. Akureyri is the capital of this region, the largest town in the north and as such, has been given a chapter to itself (chapter 8). To the east is Húsavik, another fishing town with a good hotel, which comes into its own during the winter because of its winter sports facilities. Lake Myvatn, however, is the area's greatest attraction, for its beauty, its internationally famous wildlife, and for its spectacular geological wonders (see chapter 7).

The northern coast is divided into east and west by **Eyjafjördur**, the fjord that runs inland to Akureyri. It cuts through steep-sided mountains that split the region in two. The mouth of the fjord is 24km (15 miles) wide, with the headlands of Hvannadalabjarg on the west and Gjögur on the east. The sea runs inland for almost 60km (37 miles) to Akureyri. Near Akureyri the fjord narrows to approximately

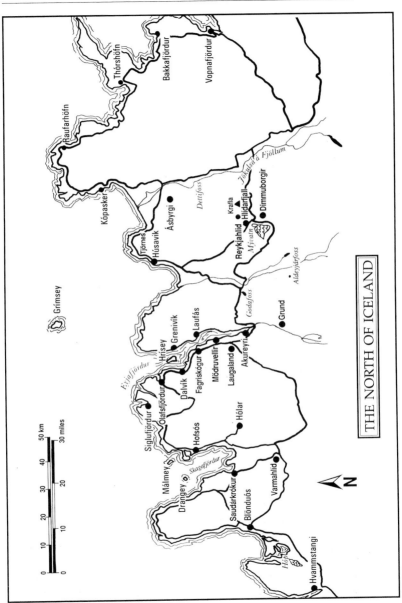

THE NORTH OF ICELAND

2½km (1½ miles) wide. The northern part around the mouth of the fjord is dominated by the mountains which fall steeply into the sea, and there is little coastal land, especially in the region between the villages of Dalvík on the western shore and Grenivík on the eastern banks. To the south, the coastal plain widens, and there are fertile plains where a wide range of crops are grown, and animals are grazed.

There are many rivers running from the fjord and it is pleasant to explore them. There are now good roads in the area, and a new one to take travellers from Akureyri across the fjord and south to Lake Myvatn is now under construction. It includes a raised section over the fjord.

Eyjafjördur is separated from the Skagafjördur Valley to the west by a range of flat-topped mountains called the Tröllaskagi, mostly between 1,200 and 1,400m (3,937 and 4,593ft) high. When driving north round the island from Reykjavík to Akureyri, the Öxnadalur Pass at 550m (1,804ft) is crossed. Another route follows the western shores of Eyjafjördur round, through the village of Ólafsfjördur, and across the high moors of the Lágheidi (400m, 1,312ft) to Siglufjördur. A tunnel then takes the route to the eastern side of Skagafjördur.

Another, smaller mountain chain is to be found between Eyjafjördur and the Skjálfandi Bay to the east, dominated by the port of Húsavik. To the south is the main road to eastern Iceland, Lake Myvatn and Reykjavík.

It is possible to drive some way up the Eyjafjördur, as far as the village of Grenivík, but beyond Grenivík the country is uninhabited and rugged, with the snow-capped coastline known as Látraströnd. Here you can see the 1,167m (3,829ft) high Kaldbakur mountain, and there are a number of small uninhabited fjords along this coast, but there is no access to them. South of Öxnadalur, which lies to the west of Akureyri, is the Kerling chain of mountains, which at 1,538m (5,046ft) provides the highest peak in northern Iceland. The range also includes the small Vindheimajökull glacier. The best winter skiing is to be found around here, especially near the Glerárdalur valley. The pyramid-shaped mountain of Súlur is another landmark.

Below Akureyri the valley gradually widens out before it climbs in altitude and is swamped by the foothills of the massive plateau which forms the uninhabited centre of the country. There are several tracks leading into the interior, including the Sprengisandur which can be used to traverse the island. It was used centuries ago by the farmers in the north, who would travel south to the fishing villages to work as part-time fishermen to eke out their living.

The area is very prosperous and there are many farms producing a wide range of crops. Many of the country's potatoes are grown here and in good years, Iceland is almost self-sufficient in this crop, but bad weather can, and often does, wipe out the entire yield.

The first settler to the Eyjafjördur is said to have been Helgi the Lean, who although a Norseman, came to Iceland via Ireland in the ninth century. Although he had been converted to Christianity he still prayed to the Scandinavian god Thor, like many of the islanders; when the island was swiftly converted to the Christian religion, most islanders simply moved their images of Norse gods into the houses and prayed to both them and their Christian God.

At the time of settlement, the valley ran much further inland, and some say Helgi came ashore at Festarklettur, a rock known now as the Mooring Rock, which is just to the south of Akureyri, while others say he chose the Gáseyri headland at the mouth of the Hörgá river, to the north of where the modern township started, to build his farmstead.

Fishing is still a major industry for the northern coastal villages, and there are fleets based at Akureyri, Hrísey Island, Dalvík, Ólafsfjördur, Siglufjördur and Grenivík. Unfortunately, the herring on which the northern fishing fleets based their economy have declined in recent years, and many of the herring processing plants in the region now lie idle.

Hrísey, the island in the mouth of Eyjafjördur, used to be the centre of shark fishing along the coast.

The whole of this region is rich in wildlife, especially as you travel southwards towards Lake Myvatn. Along the coast, however, there are important breeding grounds of the ptarmigan, Iceland's most important game bird, and some of these areas have now been closed to visitors in order to undertake research.

From the summit of Ólafsfjardarmúli there are breathtaking views northwards of the midnight sun during the summer and the island of Grímsey can be seen more than 50km (37 miles) away.

Ólafsfjördur, 63km (39 miles) from Akureyri, is a prosperous little fishing town and both its houses and swimming pool are heated by hot water from local springs. Ólafsfjördur used to be principally connected with agriculture, but since the turn of the century this has been superseded by fishing. The campsite is by the swimming pool and there is a golf course at Skeggjabrekka to the west of the town.

At the northern tip of the fjord is **Siglufjördur**, a popular tourist spot both in summer and winter, for the mountains inland provide very good skiing. Siglufjördur was once the capital of the north coast's herring industry, but declined when the fish moved away. It is now regaining its popularity, and the fisheries now process other species of fish. The town used to be known as Thormódseyri after Thórmódur the Strong, who was the first settler there. There are now two hotels, a restaurant, swimming pool, community centre and hospital. The campsite is by Ithróttamidstödin Hóll.

Dalvík is another fishing village which can trace its roots back for centuries. In olden times there were dwellings here, but they were only used by the fishermen as temporary quarters and it was not until the end of the last century that the first permanent settlers moved in. Originally the growth of the town was inhibited by the small harbour, which prevented large vessels from using it, but a new harbour was constructed shortly after the end of World War II. The people of the town pride themselves on their cultural heritage and will tell you that the first play was performed there in 1901 when there were just four families in residence. In 1934 the town was shaken by an earthquake, measuring 7.2 on the Richter Scale, 2,000 people lost their homes. There is a hotel, with the campsite alongside, and a swimming pool.

On the way down the western coast of the Eyjafjördur, there are many places of interest. The poet Davíd Stefánsson, for example, was born at a farm at **Fagriskogúr** and the historic farm at **Mödruvellir**, 12km ($7\frac{1}{2}$ miles) from Akureyri, was the site of a monastery and once one of the most important cultural and literary centres in Iceland. Other places of interest include the wooded glades of Vaglaskógur to the north-west of Akureyri and the farm of Baegisá on Öxnadalur where an Icelandic poet translated Milton's *Paradise Lost*. This area has excellent fishing.

There are many geothermal areas in the region and you can enjoy a swim at **Laugaland**.

It is possible to drive up the eastern coast of Eyjafjördur only as far as Grenivík, about 47km (29 miles) from Akureyri, but the drive is worthwhile. There is an old turf and stone manor farm at **Laufás**, on the way, and it is now a famous museum with many exhibits of national importance.

You can travel out to the island of **Grímsey**, the most northerly part of Iceland; the Arctic Circle actually runs through the island.

Blönduós (these pictures taken at 10pm)

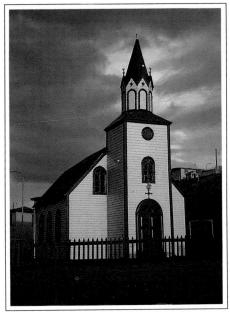

PLACES OF INTEREST IN NORTH ICELAND

Dettifoss
Most powerful waterfall in Europe.

Grímsey
Most northerly part of Iceland. The Arctic Circle runs through the island, which can be visited.

Hólar
In Hjaltadalur. Seat of the early bishops; capital of the north from 1106 to 1798. Oldest stone church in Iceland.

Húsavik
Town with many winter sports facilities.

Laufás
Old farm, now an important museum.

Ólafsfjardarmúli
Breathtaking views from summit of the midnight sun and the island of Grímsey.

Ólafsfjördur
Old fishing schooner preserved here as a memorial to one of Iceland's most celebrated ship-wrights.

Skagafjördur
Several ancient and preserved farmhouses, the best one being at Glaumbaer, including the farmer's tools, furniture, clothing etc.

Stóragjá
Caves in which there are hot pools.

Vindheimajökull
An area noted for the quality of the winter skiing.

There is sleeping bag accommodation available in the community centre, so a trip of greater length than a day can be planned.

This northern strip generally has fine, dry summers, while the winters are cold and there can be blizzards. But, like all weather guidelines, there are massive variations. Some parts of the interior, around Lake Myvatn and up to Akureyri have recently experienced their hottest summer on record, while in the winter, if the wind is blowing from the south, the temperatures around Eyjafjördur can be several degrees higher than in the south of Iceland. The rule is to go prepared with warm woollens and waterproofs for winter and light woollens and warm jacket for summer, and always swimming costumes, because no matter what the weather, there will be a hot pool somewhere.

Hvammstangi to Hofsós
(to the west of Eyjafjördur)

Hvammstangi is the only town in the western county of Húnavatn. It is a service town, and trading centre for both fishing and agricultural industries. There is a camping site close to the town, and 25km (16 miles) north-east is Hvítserkur, a 15m (49ft) high basalt rock.

Höfdakaupstadur is also called **Skagaströnd**, and is an important port. Both English and German merchants traded here before 1660 and when the trade monopoly was established in 1602 it became a major port. It has a guesthouse, a campsite by the road leading into the village, and a sports field, community centre, swimming pool, and ski lifts servicing the Spákonfell mountain which dominates the town.

The largest town in the eastern county of Húnavatn is **Blönduós**, and it has a hotel, community centre and hospital. It stands at the mouth of the glacial river Blanda and there are records of merchant ships using the harbour centuries ago. The town was granted trading rights in 1876. There is a hydro-electric project on the river close to the town. The campsite is by Nordurlandsvegur. Fishing and agriculture are the main industries.

Varmahlíd in Skagafjördur makes an excellent place to break your journey with its hotel and camping ground, swimming pool and beautiful turf-covered church at nearby Vídimyri.

The capital of Skagafjördur is **Saudárkrókur**, although the town did not exist before 1870. Its rapid expansion has taken place in the last few decades. Most of the population are involved with the fishing industry. The town has two hotels, restaurants, a campsite by the swimming pool, community centre, hospital and cinema. There is a golf course, tourist information centre and a library and art museum.

Hólar in Hjaltadalur is in Skagafjördur county; it was the seat of the early bishops and the capital of the north from 1106 to 1798. Jón Arason was bishop here in the middle of the sixteenth century, losing both his seat and his head, when he was executed along with his two sons in 1550. The church is the oldest built in stone in the country.

Hofsós is one of the oldest trading centres in Iceland, based around fishing.

Húsavík to Vopnafjördur
(to the east of Eyjafjördur)

Húsavík is a busy fishing and export harbour, with a hotel and good tourist facilities. It received its name 'House Bay' from houses built by the Swedish Viking Gardar Svavarsson, who explored Iceland before the colonisation began. There is a very unusual church which you should try to visit. There is a folk museum and tourist information centre, and the campsite is at Hédinsbraut. There is an added bonus because Húsavík also tops Iceland's sunshine league. Behind the town there is the mountain of Húsavík, and it is possible to drive up to the summit to enjoy the views. The drive takes you through the magnificent scenery of the Tjörnes peninsula.

The small town of **Kópasker** in Axarfjördur serves the local agricultural needs, but is now building up a successful fishing industry based on the shrimps found in the fjord. There is a hotel open all the year round, a restaurant, and a campsite by Söluskáli.

Raufarhöfn is very close to the Arctic Circle and an ideal site for viewing the midnight sun during the summer. It is a good birdwatching area, and there is fine salmon and trout fishing in the local rivers. There is a large hotel, community centre and swimming pool with the campsite alongside it.

Thórshöfn is a small town that is less than a hundred years old. It has a guesthouse, campsite and swimming pool. The harbour has been used for centuries as a safe anchorage but the first houses were not built until 1875 when a shop and warehouse were established. In 1900 there were seventy-five inhabitants and now the village has more than 400 residents. It is an excellent base for backpacking and walking with good trails over the surrounding heaths. The area is also rich in birdlife with large colonies along the cliffs. The locals still practise the centuries-old custom of gathering the birds eggs for food.

Vopnafjördur is mainly a fishing area, but agriculture and some other small industries also provide employment.

A Drive along the North Coast

The roads are mostly gravel but quite passable and get a lot of traffic. Hrútafjördur marks the boundary between the Western Fjords and the northern coast and almost at its head there is a motel, one of the few in Iceland, which makes a good touring base. There is an exposed campsite by the river behind the motel but the rooms are very reasonable and there is a good round-the-clock restaurant.

About 12km (7½ miles) north, along the western bank of the fjord there is a marvellous little museum at Reykjatunga, which shows just how hard life was here a few decades ago. The museum is in the Hotel Edda complex, and is the building by the water's edge to the left of the hotel. There is a modest entrance fee which includes a guide, part of which is in English. The most interesting exhibits are to do with shark fishing, the principal occupation for centuries. The men used to go to sea in open rowing boats during the shark season which lasted from mid-January until late April. Each tour lasted up to a week, only cold food was eaten and there was little chance for sleep. The bait was horse flesh and seal. The shark flesh was processed by burying it, often for years and the longer the better. The liver was processed into oil at the end of each season and used for fuel in street lamps all over Europe — a market which died after the introduction of the gas lamp. The shark boats, one of which is beautifully preserved, would have a crew of nine to thirteen men and would weigh 7 tons when fully laden.

Another fascinating exhibit is a tiny, open row boat which was used to supply groceries to the fishermen living on the other side of the fjord. In winter, the boatman would sleep on a passing iceberg with the boat's hawser tied to his left foot to stop it drifting away.

At Hvítserkur there is a strange 15m high (49ft) basalt rock, and at Borgarvirki, a crag formation and basalt column which is thought once to have been used as a fortress. On the hill top at Bakkabrúnir, remains of alder trees and other plants have been found in the top layer of clay which dates back to the Tertiary period. Just a little to the south there are very picturesque waterfalls, the Kolufossar, in Kolugil, a great gully carved through the rock by the river Vididalsá. There is a remarkable cluster of hillocks at Vatnsdalshólar, at the mouth of the Vatnsdalur Valley. They were formed after a colossal landslide from Vididalsfjall.

The island's first monastery was founded at Thingeyrar in 1133 and it became a great seat of learning and education. At Vidimyri, near to Varmahlíd, there is a well preserved turf church, and at Glaumbaer, to the north, is a lovely collection of old turf buildings, and a beautifully preserved farmstead, with the rooms still in their original state. The oldest buildings date back to the eighteenth century and the rest were added in the nineteenth century.

Ölafsfjardarmúli, to the south of Ölafsfjördur, is also worth exploring. It rises to about 400m and is famous for its perpendicular rock
belts and scree slopes. In clear weather there are excellent views of
the island of Grímsey and the midnight sun. Mödruvellir í Hörgárdal,
south, has one of the country's finest country churches built in 1868,
and the writer Nonni, otherwise known as Jón Sveinsson, and
famous worldwide for his books for young people, was born in the
parish.

South of Akureyri at Grund is Grundarkirkja, one of the most
splendid churches in Iceland. Behind it is the 1,538m (5,044ft) Kerling
mountain, the summit of which gives excellent views.

At Saurbaer there is the part turf church, now under national
protection, and at Leyningshólar, there are glacial formations of
moraines and hillocks, with scattered clusters of trees, surrounding
the lake of Tjarnargerdisvatn. The old farm at Laufás is worth visiting,
and is another national monument.

North of Myvatn is Grenjadarstadur, an ancient manor with
vicarage and church. There is also an interesting folk museum,
depicting local life of yesteryear. Tjörnes is the peninsula lying
between the bays of Skjálfandi and Öxarfjördur, with strange and
highly photogenic exposed rock strata dating back to the Iron Age.
Ásbyrgi is a natural horseshoe-shaped enclosure with impressive
rock walls towering more than 90m (295ft). Inside the enclosure there
is lush vegetation and you can camp nearby.

Jökulssárgljúfur is famous as one of the largest and most rugged
gorges in Iceland — a mini Grand Canyon, and the home of many
spectacular waterfalls including Dettifoss, Hafragilsfoss and Selfoss.
It is worth devoting some time to exploring the gorge with its caves,
eerie rock formations and creeks. It is now a national park and
camping is restricted to designated sites. **Dettifoss** is a spectacular
waterfall on the river Jökulsá about 30km (18½ miles) north-east of
Myvatn. The area in which it is situated has become the Jökulsá
Canyon National Park, and the waterfall crashes down from a height
of 44m (144ft). As you drive north from the Grímsstadir crossroads,
you follow the Jökulsá á Fjöllum on your left. The river, the country's
second longest, starts to widen its bank as it makes its way through
the gravel-lined valley. The road is boulder-strewn and can be very
muddy. The turn off on the right to Dettifoss is well signposted, but it
is best to continue along the road for about 2km (about a mile), until
you come to an unmarked track off to the left. If you follow this it will

take you to **Hafragilsfoss**, even more spectacular than Dettifoss.

There is a parking area on the crest of the hill with stunning views of the falls and the canyon. The whole area is made up of red lava, and there are a number of paths affording even better views of the falls and the canyon. It can be very windy on top of the hill so be careful. The best views of the 27m-high (88ft) falls can be got from a tall pyramid-shaped lump of lava, about 500m (1,640ft) to the left of the car park area. This is an area of canyons and water, with many gorges and rivers feeding into the main stream. The main canyon runs for 26m (85ft), and in places the sheer cliffs are more than 100m (328ft) high.

Having seen the splendours of Hafragilsfoss, you can retrace your route back to Dettifoss. The mud track to the falls can be quite slippery if it is wet, but most vehicles should manage it with care. The car park is well above the falls and as you make your way down through the rocks, the spray from the falls starts to hit you so keep your cameras protected. There is almost always a rainbow hanging over the river just to the north of the falls, and it makes for stunning photographs.

The river, which runs for 206km (127 miles), is suddenly compressed into a narrow channel which explains the ferocity of the falls. As you approach it is a good idea to keep to the path, because if you venture too near the edge you will see that the ground is rent with fissures, and every so often a chunk of cliff slides down into the canyon.

The Dettifoss falls are 45m (146ft) high and the flow of water, up to 1,500cu m (52,931cu ft) a second, makes it the most powerfall in Europe. It is possible to walk upstream for about a kilometre to the much smaller Selfoss (13m, 42ft) although the path is boulder-strewn and not easy to follow.

A Drive From Egilsstadir to Myvatn

Driving in the eastern part of this region can be one of the great adventures of a trip to Iceland. If you leave Egilsstadir, over the wooden bridge and past the airport, the routes to Myvatn and Akureyri are well signposted. You travel through Fellabaer where you can go horse riding, and into lush green sheep pastures. It is worth a stop just beyond the bridge which crosses the Jökulsá á Brú, and walking back to see how the waters have carved out a deep canyon.

A threatening sky over Brautarholt Farm near Varmahlíd

The ring road heads roughly north and then swings south-west. Gradually the vegetation becomes more sparse, the number of abandoned farms increase and you get the feeling that you are heading out into a remote and desolate area.

Here the river has carved its way through hills of gravel, brought down over the centuries from Brúarjökull, a northern arm of Vatnajökull. In some places the gravel is tens of metres deep and it is grassing over, offering sparse grazing for the sheep. On the right there are steep cliffs and waterfalls, and you pass only a few very isolated farms. It is always a good idea to fill up with fuel when you get the chance, and there is a pump at Skjöldólfsstadir. After crossing the river Gilsá, the road starts to climb into the mountains before forking. You should take the right fork, still on the ring road and signposted to Myvatn and Akureyri.

The landscape is even more barren, with moss-covered rocks, lava and black sand. In the summer the brown and black colours can be broken by a burst of multi-coloured alpine flowers. Beside the roads there are cairns, a reminder of days gone by when this was the only means of navigating. This area is notorious for dust storms and they can blow up very quickly, catching you unawares.

It is a lonely road with few vehicles, but you will spot the approach of another car miles away because of the dust it throws up. The road crosses this flat lava desert known as Geitasandur, and as you start to descend, you can see the even more imposing desert of Grjót in the valley below. The road heads north skirting the eastern flank of the desert, past Mödrudalur, at 469m (1,538ft) the highest farm in Iceland, until it hits Grimsstadir, and then you can either head south on Route 864 to visit Dettifoss, or west on Route 1 to Myvatn and Akureyri.

If you have a four-wheel drive vehicle and plan to drive to Askja, the road leads off south from the ring road, 7km (4 miles) after the Grimsstadir crossroad. Before making the journey, however, call in at the farmhouse at Grimsstadir and find out what the conditions are like and what the weather forecast is. There is a campsite opposite the farm with toilets and washing facilities, and is a good base for exploring north along the Route 864, if you don't want to have to keep retracing the road back to Myvatn.

7

LAKE MYVATN AND THE SURROUNDING AREA

T he area around Lake Myvatn is not only Iceland's most beautiful
countryside, but some of its most interesting. It is a geological
paradise and everywhere has something new and exciting to see.

Lake Myvatn is the fifth largest lake in Iceland, with an area of
about 37sq km (14sq miles) and it lies 278m (912ft) above sea level.
The lake has literally hundreds of inlets and creeks, each one the
home of ducks and waders. The lake is in two parts — Ytritflói and
Sydriflói. The average depth is only 2.5m (9ft) and the maximum
depth is 4.5m (15ft). There are more than fifty islands, and the largest
are clusters of pseudo-craters — explosion craters formed by hot
lava flowing into the lake. Almost all the water flowing into the lake
comes from springs along the eastern shore. The river Graenilaekur,
which flows from the spring-fed Lake Graenavatn in the south, is the
only surface flowing stream of any note running into Myvatn.

There are more varieties of duck on Lake Myvatn than anywhere
else in the world, which is why it is of such importance to ornithologists. Geologically it is very interesting because the land is so new.
It is actually being altered all the time, and eruptions occur frequently,
although few are violent. In the last few years, however, the amount
of geo-thermal activity has increased enormously, and there are now
many columns of steam rising from fissures to the north and east of

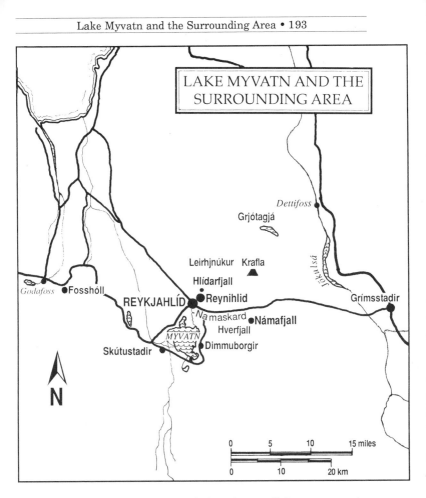

LAKE MYVATN AND THE
SURROUNDING AREA

Dettifoss

Grjótagjá

Leirhjnúkur   Krafla

Hlídarfjall

Godafoss ●Fosshóll   ●Reynihlid   Grímsstadir

REYKJAHLÍD

Namaskard ●Námafjall
            Hverfjall

MYVATN

Skútustadir   ●Dimmuborgir

N

Jökulsá

0	5	10	15 miles
0		10	20 km

the lake. Experts are convinced that there will be more major eruptions here but they cannot say how soon.

The lake gets its name from the midges and black-flies which can prove a nuisance in summer. At certain times the midges swarm and unless you are well protected, it is almost impossible to breathe without inhaling large numbers into your nose and mouth. It is only the female black-fly that bites, and usually only in damp and calm weather. They are not supposed to bite indoors! The presence of the midges give a clue to the area's climate; in the lee of the Vatnajökull

Lake Myvatn

glacier it gets little rain, making it one of the driest and sunniest places in Iceland. Summer temperatures of over 20˚C (68˚F) have often been recorded, and summers often consist of many warm, dry days strung together. Annual rainfall is about 40cm (16in), ten times less than on the glacier to the south. Because of its position and climate, Lake Myvatn is considered to be the most fertile place of any on its latitude.

The district was formed about 3,800 years ago from the older Laxá lava, and lava flows have been adding to it ever since. In some places the earth's crust is only inches thick, and many unsuspecting people have been badly burned by breaking the surface; their feet having been scalded by the underlying hot sulphur pools, so please follow the notices in these areas which advise travellers of where to walk in safety.

The lake in the summer plays host to up to 150,000 ducks as well as thousands of geese and waders. The Barrow's goldeneye, an American species, is found nowhere else in Europe, and the harlequin, also a North American native, does not breed anywhere east of Iceland. The most common duck to be seen is the scaup. There are approximately 3,500 pairs of tufted duck, 1,800 pairs of scaup, 1,000 pairs of wigeon and 500 pairs of Barrow's goldeneye.

There are red-breasted merganser, common scoter, long-tailed duck, mallard, and teal, and less frequently gadall, pintail, shoveller, and goosander. Large numbers of eider breed along the Laxá, and about 600 whooper swans choose the lake to moult. There are numerous horned grebe, red necked phalarope, great northern and red throated divers, greylag geese, gyr falcons, ptarmigan, assorted plovers, gulls and terns. There are also snow buntings, pied wagtail, wheatear, raven and redwing. Mink which escaped into the wild, were first seen in the 1960s but are now common, while the arctic fox has become rare. The other animal to be seen is the long-tailed field mouse which is plentiful. The birds are protected by law, and the countryside is protected by the Icelanders ever mindful of the wonders of Myvatn which they hold in trust for mankind. One writer described Myvatn as an open book detailing the world's creation. Arctic char live in the lake and trout migrate from Laxá so that they can spawn near the springs on the eastern side of the lake. A dwarf char has evolved which lives in subterranean caves and the three-spined stickleback is very common. Salmon migrate up the Laxá in the spring.

Myvatn is a paradox, because it is a small area, with enormous contrasts, in which one can get lost because it is unspoilt and unpopulated. Here the vegetation is strange, and on the newest lava there is no vegetation at all. This is the wonder of Myvatn; the land is so new that it is possible to watch the evolution of land through its various stages, from bare new lavafields to those which have been colonised, first by moss and lichens, then by plants and shrubs, and then finally by the squat Icelandic trees. The most luxuriant growth will usually be found inside the crevices, where the plants get maximum protection from the weather and enjoy their own freak micro-climate.

The vegetation around Myvatn and the Laxá river running from it is particularly lush and contains many rare plants; there is even one named the Queen of Myvatn. There are birch woodlands to the north and east of the lake, and bogs and moors to the south and west. Bottle sedge forms many of the reed beds, while the string sedge dominates the marshy areas. Other vegetation includes dwarf birch, tea-leaved willows, and willow. There is angelica and meadow buttercup, marsh marigold and wood cranesbill. Lichens are very common and the vegetation of the lake includes two species of watermilfoil, the water crowfoot and sago pondweed. Because of the algae in the lake, the water often turns opaque blue-green in July. Other common vascular plants in the area include: woolly willow, sorrel, alpine mouse-ear, hairy stonecrop, marsh cinquefoil, water and mountain avens, field gentian, thyme, butterwort, ladies' bedstraw, boreal fleabane and yarrow. The lake itself is shallow, and in places is edged by reed beds and small marshy areas. In most places it is between 1 and 3m (3 to 7ft) deep.

Two types of midges live around the lake, the true midge, and the black-fly which is a real scourge as it is the only one which bites. In some summers thick clouds composed of hundreds of thousands of midges can be seen, and for some reason, they travel to only one or two special islands to die. These islands are much greener with vegetation than the others because they are being fertilised by the bodies of millions of midges. Scientists do not yet know why the midges should choose these particular islands on which to die. Some midges die before they reach either of the islands and drop into the water. They help fertilise the marine plant life which attracts the birds, and so the cycle continues.

The area has been protected by the country's Nature Conserva-

River Laxá

tion Council since 1974 and is considered by the World Wildlife Fund to be one of the most important bird habitats on earth. There is also a research centre at Reykjahlíd run by the Nordic Volcanological Institute.

There are less than 600 people living in the area, and farming is the main occupation as it has been for centuries. Tourism, however, is becoming very important and facilities to cope with the growing number of visitors are being provided. Again, however, it must be stressed that although tourism is growing for obvious reasons, there are no crowds. There is so much open space, and the number of visitors at any one time is still relatively small, so it is possible to spend whole days and see only a handful of people. Most of the population is concentrated at Reykjahlíd with its hotels, camping site and other services.

Most of the farmers raise sheep which graze along the edges of the lake, but there is excellent fishing in this area, and this has helped supplement the diets of the local people, as have eggs from the nesting water birds. Although agriculture is now the major industry, there are others.

Hafragilsfoss

Mining, especially, has played a role in the region for centuries. Hundreds of years ago there were sulphur mines here; as this industry died out, the lava came into its own. It was taken to factories where it was crushed and pressed into building blocks, and there are still plants doing this today. The major mining enterprise, however, is the plant which opened in 1966. It extracts the mineral from material dredged up from the shallow bed of Lake Myvatn. Diatomite is used in a number of industrial processes, including making photographic film. Because of the growing popularity of the area there is quite a lot of building work going on in the towns, and the construction industry is the second largest industrial employer after the mining.

As you travel into the area from the west, especially in the Fnjóskárdalur Valley, remnants of the birch forests that once covered the whole of northern Iceland can be seen. In the Ljósavatn Pass, which passes through the basalt mountain range, there are the remnants of a massive earthslip from the Stóradalsfjall mountain, which took place at the end of the Ice Age after the ice had melted. On the journey from Akureyri to the lake, a convenient stop is at the farm at **Ljósavatn**, where Thorgeir Godi, the warrior priest lived. It was he who, in AD1000, decreed that Iceland should change to

Christianity, and that the Nordic idols should be thrown out. Around this farm the landscape changes away from jagged mountains and plunging valleys to the lavafields and moors, and glacial hills that make up the scenery of Myvatn.

There is the lava of **Bárdardalur**, already clad in shrubs and mosses, which came 8,000 years ago from the Trölladyngjur. It is the longest shield volcano lavafield in Iceland, running for over 100km (62 miles).

The Myvatn moor is dominated in the south by the tall volcanic mountains, and the special colouring on Námafjall caused by the hot springs and sulphur wells is striking. It was here that the sulphur was mined in the Middle Ages.

All around, the landscape is marked by the effects of glaciers, earthquakes and volcanoes, but the view is dominated by the volcano, Krafla.

Arnarbaeli is a closed lava knoll just by the road to the south of Myvatn and east of Skutustadir. From the road it looks like a small solid hill, but from the top it can be seen that the structure is hollow. There is also a pseudo-crater beside the road.

Dimmuborgir is a large lava pile east of Myvatn, now rich in plant life and with many trees. Known to the locals as the Land of Dark Castles, the lava has been formed and eroded into many strange and wonderful shapes, many of which look as if they have been built by man. There are caves and holes in the cliff; the most famous cave is known as the Church of the Fortress (Kirkjan) and it has what appears to be a large Gothic-style vault.

Many of the lava formations tower 15 to 25m (49 to 82ft) high; and were formed by lava-flow some 2,000 years ago. The younger Laxá lava came from Threngslaborgir which can be seen from the small hill as you enter the enclosure. The castles, best viewed just before sunset, are at their finest near Valsbjarg which has become a nesting-place for falcons. It is possible to spend several hours in this fascinating area of lava architecture which is enclosed behind a fence. Although there are footpaths it is very easy to get lost; if this happens, do not cross the fence, but simply follow it around until the only gate is reached.

The area of lava between Reykjahlíd and Grímsstadir that flowed from Leirhnjúkur during the Myvatn Fires of 1729 is called **Eldhraun**. The flow extends for several kilometres.

Grjótagjá is the name of a ground fissure to the east of Myvatn that runs for several kilometres. There are many pools in the fissure, and they get warmer the farther to the north they are. Many of the pools used to be popular for bathing, but since the volcanic activity in the area has considerably increased, they have now become too hot to swim in.

About 4km (2½ miles) to the north-east of Reykjahlíd is a cone-shaped mountain called **Hlídarfjall**. It is 771m (2,529ft) high, and forms a good vantage point to survey the surrounding countryside. **Hverfjall** is claimed to be the most famous crater in the Myvatn region. It was formed about 2,500 years ago during an explosive eruption and there is now a large tuff ring to be seen east of Myvatn. It is more than one kilometre across and rises about 150m (492ft) above the surrounding land. It is called 'the perfect mountain' because its shape is so symmetrical.

There is an area of unusual lava flow running eastwards from Myvatn towards Kálfastrandarvogur called **Höfdi**. It is considered to be one of the most beautiful spots beside the lake. For many years it has been a public park because of its rich vegetation and strange lava shapes. This whole area is well worth a visit and is a paradise for photographers.

Jardbadshólar has a steam bath where locals have taken healing baths for centuries. Kálfastrandarstrípar, near Höfdi, a short walk away, is also worth exploring because of its strangely-shaped lava rocks. The reason for the strange formations is that there was once a lava pool here whose level suddenly dropped, leaving behind lava columns that solidified.

About 10km (6 miles) north-east of Myvatn, the great volcano, **Krafla**, has become a regular tourist attraction because of its frequent eruptions. The latest and most powerful in recent years occurred in September 1984 when a 9km (5½ mile) long fissure opened up and lava started to flow. The force of the eruption was so great that at about 2am it could be seen more than 300km (186 miles) away, lighting up the sky.

The central volcano is 20km (12 miles) wide, and the caldera is about 8km (5 miles) in diameter. A large fissure runs north and south about the caldera, and there is thought to be a magma chamber underneath the centre of the caldera about 7km (4 miles) down. Its longest eruption ever took place during the 5 years from 1724, when so much lava flowed that at the time it became known as the Myvatn Fires. In 1975 volcanic activity started again, and there has been an

Dettifoss

eruption every year since, although some have lasted for only a few hours, while others rumbled on for some days. At the same time there have been a number of earth tremors in this area which have caused land movements and earth slips. There is some concern at the increased activity because a hugely expensive geothermal power station has been built on Krafla, and the first of the recent eruptions occurred during the first year of construction.

Laxá is a magnificent river rising in Lake Myvatn and flowing north for about 50km (31 miles) to the sea. It is one of Iceland's most popular salmon rivers and between 1954 and 1963 more than 1,150 salmon, with an average weight of 10lb, were caught annually. A new fishing lodge has been built on the river, at which it is possible to stay on full board or self-catering terms. A bed can be obtained at a cost which is insignificant in comparison with what is paid on some of the top English and Welsh rivers.

There is a large geothermal area to the west of Krafla called **Leirhjnúkur**, dominated by a rounded volcanic hill. You can see a variety of craters and boiling mud holes, or mudpots, and the area is carpeted with flowers in the summer. The ground is so warm that spring comes here earlier almost than anywhere else in Iceland, even though it is 600m (1,970ft) above sea level.

Lúdent is a large crater about 6km (3½ miles) east of Myvatn, and formed more than 6,000 years ago. It is almost 1km (1,000yd) wide and to the south and east you can see a number of spatter cones that stretch for many kilometres. The area is known as Lúdentsborgir.

There is another geothermal area called **Námaskard**, and here caution must be exercised when walking round it — the earth's crust is only inches thick, and so it is essential to keep to the areas indicated. There are bubbling mudpots, sulphur wells and hot springs. The earth is multi-coloured because of the sulphur and other chemicals in it. You can cross from the road, through the geothermal area to Námafjall which rises to 482m (1,580ft), and there are excellent views from the top of the mountain. Just beyond this area is the first geothermal plant, built in 1968, and the diatomite plant.

Neslandavík is a shallow cove, almost 3km (1½ miles) long and up to 1km (1,000yd) wide, in the north-west shore of Lake Myvatn. It is one of the best breeding grounds in the area and has been proclaimed a nature reserve, so no cars are permitted on the road here between 15 May and 20 July.

There is a 20sq km (7¾sq mile) area north of Reykjahlíd called

Reykjahlídarheidi full of kettle holes and moraines, and overgrown with birch, willow and rowan. It was formed about 10,000 years ago, by water when the glaciers melted at the end of the last Ice Age. In winter it is ideal for cross-country skiing.

Reykjahlíd is the tourist centre for the region with hotels and campsites. According to legend, the first man to live here was Arnór Thorgrímsson. There is believed to have been a church on the hill overlooking the town ever since the country turned to Christianity in AD1000. During the Myvatn Fires on 21 August 1729, lava from Eldhraun flowed round the church, and although it piled up against the walls, it did not enter the building. The foundations of that old church are still preserved, although there have been two churches on the site since then, the last being built in 1962.

In Reykjahlíd town there is a lava core called Saudahellir, it is about 70m (230ft) long, and in places it is tall enough for a person to stand upright. It is named after the sheep which used to be sheltered here, although it is now used as a potato store.

West of Bláfjall there is a breathtaking ravine called **Seljahallagil**, about 7km (4¼ miles) south-east of Myvatn. There are magnificent columnar basalt formations at the end, formed when a lava flow entered the ravine about 3,800 years ago.

Skútustadagígar is an area of pseudo-craters beside the lake. They can be inspected but visitors are asked to keep to the clearly marked footpaths. Pseudo-craters are formed when lava flows into a lake or waterlogged area. The heat of the lava causes the water below to boil, and steam bursts through. Cinders and ash are forced up thus building the craters. It was here, at Thangbrand's Pool, in 998, that a German missionary baptised the inhabitants of Myvatn into the Christian religion.

A large number of nesting birds can be seen at **Slútnes**, which is a lowland and fertile island in the north-east corner of Myvatn.

Stóragjá is another fissure to the south of Reykjahlíd which used to have pools popular with bathers. Again, the waters have become considerably hotter with the recent volcanic action, and bathing is no longer advised. **Sydrivogar** is a variegated lava cove in the south-east corner of Lake Myvatn. The water comes mainly from the freshwater springs along the east shore. **Vindbelgur** is a volcanic mountain about 240m (78ft) high, west of Myvatn and about a mile from the road. There is an easy path up the west side, and it is worth the climb for the views from the top. About 5km (3 miles) south-east

Jökulsá Canyon National Park

Godafoss

of Myvatn there is **Threngslaborgir**, an 8½km (5¼ mile) long row of spatter and scoria cones. There are water-filled craters, and some fissures are so deep and sheltered that snow is trapped here throughout the summer.

The attractions of the area for the ornithologist are obvious but there are strict rules preventing the birds being disturbed between 15 May and 20 July. Boats can be hired for trips on the lake, for fun or for fishing. Fishing permits for the Laxá are sold in Arnarvatn, and fishing is also allowed on Myvatn, where there are char.

The area is a walker's paradise and there are many local trails, although few have been waymarked. In the winter there is good cross-country skiing, and of course, there is all-the-year-round swimming in some of the hot pools. There are regular flights from Reykjavík to either Akureyri or Húsavik, and a shuttle bus runs from the latter to Myvatn in the summer. There is an airstrip at Reykjahlíd, and small planes can land there, opposite the hotel. During the summer, there are bus trips to Myvatn from Reykjavík travelling over the interior highlands. There are daily summer buses between Akureyri and Myvatn, and four trips a week between Húsavik and

Myvatn, although during the summer peak period, there are daily trips. There are also three trips during the summer between Myvatn and Egilsstadir.

There are many tours organised in and around Myvatn taking in all the places of interest. Details can be obtained from hotels, travel agents, Icelandair, or Eldá Lake Myvatn (which runs many of them).

The Myvatn area has its own cuisine, with trout and lamb as the favourite dishes. Reindeer, which roam the eastern highlands is often offered on the menu. The locals bake a rye bread in the volcanic earth and it goes particularly well with smoked trout. There is also *grasamjólk*, a rather special dessert made from milk and Icelandic moss.

One other delicacy, which may not appeal, is rotten eggs. The locals gather them in the spring, and bury them in ashes before hardboiling them. They are eaten for Thorrablót, the traditional late January feast, and are said to taste like ripe cheese!

When it is time to leave Myvatn and head for Akureyri stop off at **Godafoss**, another of Iceland's wonders. From Reykjahlíd drive south down the western shore of Myvatn on Route 1. The road then turns north-westerly, past Másvatn and on to Einarsstadir. Stay on the ring road until Fosshóll where the river is bridged. It is possible to approach the falls on either side of the road, down the east bank on the 844 and the west bank using the 842. The west bank has the better car park, but the east bank gives the best views. The 10m-high (33ft) falls carry huge volumes of water and are known as the Falls of the Gods, because when Iceland adopted Christianity, the deed was celebrated by the symbolic casting of the pagan gods into the waters of the falls.

8

AKUREYRI: THE JEWEL OF THE NORTH

A kureyri, the third largest town in Iceland, nestles between mountains on an inlet on the northern shore of Iceland. On fine days you can see ships at sea that are inside the Arctic Circle, yet the town, the largest in the north, enjoys a warm climate, frequently with hot summers.

For almost 500 years, the perfect natural harbour attracted trading ships, but it was not until 1777 that the town began to grow. In 1785 the official register still only recorded ten inhabitants, all of them Danish.

The river mouth, which was originally used as the harbour, gradually silted up, and the trading post was moved to the end of the fjord, in the shelter of the Oddeyri peninsula. Shops, warehouses and stockpens for animals were built, but it was not until the late eighteenth century that Akureyri really became established. This was at the time of the repressive Danish trading laws and the King of Denmark ordained that all merchants with trading monopolies in Iceland must live there.

Due to this decree, Friarik Lynge built his home near the warehouses, and the first home in Akureyri was thus erected. The first house on the Oddeyri peninsula was built in about 1858, and within 8 years this district had been merged with the now established

A view of Akureyri

PLACES OF INTEREST IN AKUREYRI

Akureyrarkirkja
The Lutheran State Church
The church was completed in 1940 and was designed by Gudjón Samúelsson, the architect of many of Iceland's finest buildings. One of the decorated stone frames came from Coventry Cathedral which was destroyed during World War II. Services are conducted June to September every Sunday at 11am and October to May at 2pm.

Amtsbókasafnid
The Municipal Library
Established in 1827 and operated by the municipality since 1906, the library contains 83,000 volumes. The archives was founded in 1967 and contains documents about the town, its institutions and families.

Davídshus
Davíd Stefánsson Memorial House
The house was built in 1944 by the Poet Stefánsson (1895-1964) and he lived there until his death. The house contains his personal property, including his personal library, and it remains in the condition he left it.

Fridbjarnarhus
The Order of Good Templars Museum
The house was built in 1856. The first IOGT order in Iceland, the Order of Isafold No 1, was founded in the building on 10 January 1884. The house is now a museum preserving many of the objects used in the activities of the Order.

Lystigardur Akureyri
Botanical Gardens
Founded in 1912, the gardens present living samples of what can be grown in northern latitudes. A living collection of almost all Iceland's native plants has been maintained since 1957. Most of the 2,000 plant species on display are labelled.

Akureyri. The town received its charter as a trading post in 1862 when the population is believed to have been about 286. Since then it has grown gradually, and now has about 14,000 inhabitants.

Because of its close links with trading ships from Denmark, Akureyri was very similar to many Danish villages, and this character and charm was preserved for many years, but unfortunately, little remains today. However, Akureyri's roots as a trading settlement still

Minjasafnid
The Municipal Museum
The museum illustrates what life used to be like in Akureyri and area, with exhibits of work tools, culture and art. There are splendid examples of artistic needlework by the womenfolk, their unique national costume, as well as fine silver work and wood carvings by the men. An old church, dating from 1846 stands next to the museum and is open during the same hours.

Náttúrugripasafnid
The Akureyri Natural History Museum
Founded in 1951 it houses extensive collections of Icelandic and European plants, animals from Iceland and a world-wide collection of sea shells. It is a centre for mycology (the study of fungi) in the area. The oldest and most complete collection is a display of native birds and eggs, containing all the country's nesting birds. The flora of the country is represented in a series of pressed plants arranged in folders.

Nonnahus
The childhood home of Nonni, the Reverend Jón Sveinsson (1857-1944) a Jesuit priest and writer of children's books which have been translated into more than forty languages. The house was opened to the public as a museum on the 100th anniversary of his birth. It displays copies of his books, and their translations, as well as original illustrations. The house is one of the older properties in the town, built in 1850.

Sigurhaedir
Matthías Jochumsson Memorial House
The house of the national poet and pastor who lived from 1835-1920. He had the house built in 1902 and lived in it until his death. He composed the words for the Icelandic National Anthem, and translated many of the works of Shakespeare and Shelley. The house contains some of his personal property and his literary works.

remain and it is the centre for the very prosperous northern region. The town houses most of the commercial and service needs of the region, and has a thriving port and shipyard.

In 1870 the Grána Trading Company was founded in Akureyri, as a co-operative business, and for many years it was the most successful commercial enterprise in Iceland with branches in many districts. At the height of its prosperity the company was based in

Akureyri cathedral

*Main shopping
street, Akureyri*

Oddeyri. When the company began to lose its influence, it was replaced by the Akureyri Co-operative Society (KEA). The Society opened the first general store owned by the Association of Icelandic Co-operatives (SIS) in Akureyri in 1906 and for many years it has been the largest and most successful co-operative in the country.

While the rich land to the south contributes to the prosperity of farming, the richness of the sea is also another factor in Akureyri's success. It has long had a fishing fleet and its herring factories were once famous. The herring salting factory at Krossanes was built by the Norwegians, but bought by the town in 1946 and has been run by the municipal authorities since then. Herring is still caught, and salted, or processed, but the decline in the catch has hit the industry.

For the last 130 years Akureyri has also been a thriving industrial centre. Records show that in 1853, when there were only 230 inhabitants, Akureyri had a printer, a bookbinder, four gold and silversmiths, five carpenters, one saddler, one mason and one cobbler apart from several others who were part-time tradesmen.

Today there are many more industries as diverse as bakeries and breweries, candy makers and shipbuilding. The shipyard is the largest in Iceland.

Akureyri also has a thriving cultural life, and the national poet Matthías Jochumsson, who lived in the town for 34 years, said, 'Schools are and will be crucial in endowing this town with the aura of a capital, success and respect'. It is perhaps because of this that Akureyri is known not only as the 'Jewel of the North', but also as the 'Capital of the North'.

A visit to Akureyri is essential for anyone who wants to see the 'other Iceland'. It is only 45 minutes flying time away from Reykjavík and the flight alone, over mountains and glaciers, is well worth it.

It seems strange to see beautifully coloured gardens in Akureyri, with snow-capped mountains beyond, but the people have always taken a pride in their gardens, and even though the summer is relatively short they always seem to produce a marvellous array of flowers.

The ease with which one can get to Akureyri can also be a blessing when one remembers that the weather in the south is often the exact opposite to that in the north.

Although Akureyri and its surrounding area sees a lot of snow during the winter, the summers are generally mild, and there can be spells of several days of hot, windless weather. The 1984 summer will go on record as one of the hottest ever, with temperatures on some days rivalling those of the Mediterranean. It is this warm summer weather, and the town's love of gardening, that led to the opening in 1912 of the town's park. It began as the idea of a few townswomen, but now has an important place as a living collection of Iceland's flora. The collection contains a specimen of every flower and plant that grows in the country.

Because of Akureyri's growing popularity as a tourist centre, there has been a determined effort to provide more accommodation and now there are hotels and hostels to suit all needs. There are also three campsites, two on the outskirts of the town and one by the pool. Akureyri is worth visiting not only in its own right, but because it is the perfect springboard for discovering the rest of the region, especially Lake Myvatn.

In the winter, the area is also popular with skiers, and Iceland's main winter sports centre is to be found near Akureyri. On the mountain slopes above the town at Hlídarfjall, there are ski slopes

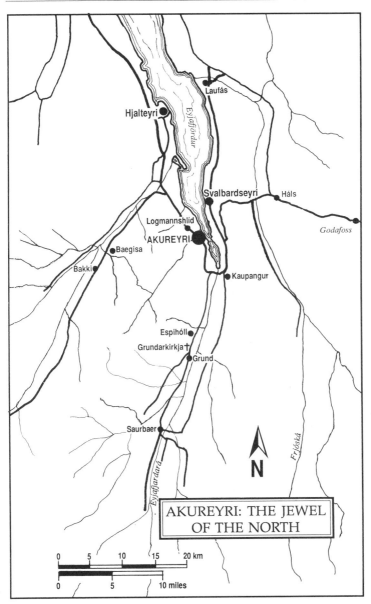

AKUREYRI: THE JEWEL
OF THE NORTH

both for experts and beginners, with a modern ski hotel and lifts.

The tops of the mountains are capped with snow all year round and it is possible to ski here during the summer if you are experienced. During the winter the best skiing is between 500m and 1,000m (1,640ft and 3,280ft) above sea level, about $11\frac{1}{4}$km (7 miles) out of town. There are heavy falls of snow from mid-December right through to the end of May. A bus service runs three times a day from the centre of town.

The ski hotel, which is at an altitude of 500m (1,640ft), has eleven double rooms, and sleeping bag accommodation for up to seventy people. There is a sauna to get rid of the day's aches and pains, and ski equipment can be hired. The hotel is open during the peak season, from January to May; it also offers ski instruction. The longest lift goes up to the 1,000m (3,280ft) level, and the longest slope down runs for about 3km (1.8 miles). All the ski routes are compressed by snow tractors, and are floodlit during the evenings for the romantics. There is some marvellous walking in this area, and many walks can be started from the hotel. They are waymarked.

During the summer months, there is still a lot of sport to be had in Akureyri. Like everywhere else in Iceland, swimming is very popular and the town pool is open from June to the end of September. There is a good golf course on the outskirts of the town, and pony trekking trips, on the sturdy Icelandic ponies, are available and becoming increasingly popular.

There are ten restaurants, four dance halls and a disco and the usual shops and facilities. You can wander around several museums, visit the public library, enjoy a sauna, go to the cinema or theatre, or loosen up at one of the town's ten athletic clubs. Like all Icelanders, the people of Akureyri love football and hold matches at one of four grounds. In addition there are six community centres, most of which visitors are made welcome. Akureyri church is noted for its stained glass windows.

There are four or five flights a day between Reykjavík and Akureyri during the summer and three or four flights daily over the winter months. Flights are operated four to five times a week to the following localities in eastern Iceland: Vopnafjördur, Raufarhöfn, Thórshöfn, and Kópasker. From the east coast: Seydisfjördur-Egilsstadir-Akureyri daily except Sundays. There is a daily flight to the Western Fjords (Isafjördur) except Sundays. There are five to six flights a week to Ólafsfjördur, Siglufjördur and Grímsey. There is a

regular bus service to the south and east and to the villages north of
Akureyri: Dalvík, Ólafsfjördur, Hrísey and Árskógsströnd to Hrísey.

Some of Iceland's most beautiful places are to be found around
Akureyri. One can travel to see the old farm at Laufás and the old-
style church at Saurbaer in the valley south of Akureyri. At Grund
there is another unusual church which looks as if it has been built
along Byzantine architectural lines. Across the mountain to the east
there is the famous waterfall, Godafoss, on the way to Lake Myvatn,
which is rapidly becoming one of the country's most popular resorts.
The whole area to the south and east of Akureyri is volcanic and
eruptions can be expected at almost any time. While there have not
been any eruptions in recent years that have been dangerous to life,
there have been some quite spectacular things to see including the
volcano Krafla.

All these places are explored more fully in chapters 6 and 7.

9

GREENLAND

Greenland is the world's largest island, and just a hop across the water from Iceland, so if you have time, or can make it, a visit is well worthwhile. The island covers 2,175,600sq km (840,000sq miles), of which almost 80 per cent is covered by ice. If ever there was a case for two islands swapping their name, this was it.

About 50,000 Greenlanders live on the island, a mixture of Eskimos and Europeans, almost all living along the southern and eastern coastal strip or on offshore islands. The biggest town is Godthab on the south-west coast, which has about 9,000 inhabitants.

It is possible to fly to Greenland from Iceland but any visit must be planned carefully. Flights are frequently cancelled because of bad weather, and it is not unusual to be stranded in Greenland for 24 hours or more. If this delay comes at the end of your holiday it could mean missing your return flight home. Stopovers because of delays are usually the responsibility of the passenger, so ensure you have extra cash with you. If visiting Greenland on a day trip, warm clothing and stout boots must be worn. If planning a longer trip, more detailed arrangements will have to be made. Communities are small and isolated, and the main methods of internal transport are by plane and helicopter, while boats ply around the coast.

Greenland enjoys home rule — ever since May 1979 — within the Kingdom of Denmark. Greenlandic is the mother tongue, although many people speak Danish and English. Danish coinage is the legal

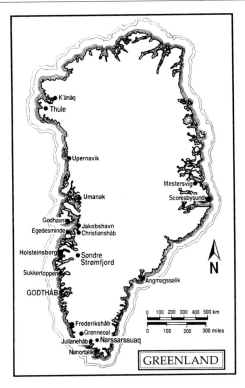

K'änáq
Thule

Upernavik

Mestersvig
Umanak
Scoresbysund

Godhavn
Jakobshavn
Egedesminde
Christianshåb

Holsteinsborg
Søndre
Strømfjord

Sukkertoppen

GODTHÅB

Angmagssalik

N

0 100 200 300 400 500 km

0   100   200   300 miles

Frederikshåb
Grønneoal
Julianehåb   Narssarssuaq
Nanortalik

GREENLAND

currency. Greenland's links with Denmark date back to 1721 when the Danish missionary Hans Egede arrived to spread Christianity, although it was the Norwegian Viking Eirík the Red who first landed there in AD985. Having already been banished from Norway for feuding, he was serving 3 years' exile from Iceland when he discovered this land of ice. He called it Greenland in a bid to attract settlers, and the Norse colonists survived until the sixteenth century when the change in the weather meant crops could no longer grow. Traces of these settlements can still be seen today.

The traditional occupation of sealing has now been replaced by agriculture and other methods of fishing. Sheep and reindeer are the main livestock. There are minerals on the island but a cryolite mine, important during World War II, is now worked out, and a coal mine which opened in 1924 was closed in 1972 because it was no longer

PLACES TO VISIT IN GREENLAND

Angmagssalik

Just across the fjord from Kulusuk and is an Eskimo settlement. It was discovered by a Danish naval expedition in 1884 led by Gustav Holm, who were making their way along the east coast in rowing boats made from skins stretched over a wooden framework. There were 413 inhabitants, but when a second expedition returned 8 years later the number had fallen to 294, the lack of seals having led to chronic starvation. Today it is east Greenland's largest town with about 1,000 inhabitants, while a further 1,500 make their living from fishing and seal hunting in the seven surrounding villages of Ikateq (Murky Waters), Isortoq, Quernertuarssuitt (Black Mountains), Kungmuit (River Dwellers), Tiniteqilaq (Dry Sound), Sermiligaq (Beautiful Glacier Fjord), and Kulusuk.

The settlement is 30km (18 miles) from Kulusuk airport, and there are regular helicopter flights between the two. Tours here normally include a guided helicopter tour of the area. You can also fly over the ice cap, and there are a number of walking tours. From March to May there are a limited number of dog sledge and ski tours. All special equipment is provided together with a hunter guide and cooking staff. The tours are based at Hotel Angmagssalik, the town's only hotel.

Godthab

(Greenland name Nyuk)
The island's largest town and the administration centre with 9,000 inhabitants. Peole have lived on the site for as long as the island has been inhabited, and there are still the remains of early Norse and Eskimo settlements. The present town was founded in 1728 by the missionary Hans Egede, and his house survives today. The old town has changed little since those days. There are hotels, restaurants, banks, shops, hospital, teachers' training college, national library and national museum. There are also outfitters where you can hire clothing, camping gear and fishing equipment and guides for trips.

Holsteinsborg

(Greenland name Sisimuit)
The island's second largest town, with a population of around 3,500. It is built on hilly terrain near the Polar Circle in a region which is free of ice nearly all the year. In 1756 a colony was founded just north of the town at Sydbay and within 8 years had spread to take in the present site. It was a centre for the whale industry, and today is still heavily involved with fishing, and has one of Greenland's most modern fleets. The first church, built in 1773, is still standing and well preserved, as are a number of

the town's original buildings, including the Old House dating from 1756, and the Governor's House built in 1846. The town has the island's only high school, and a large shipbuilding yard. There is a hotel and hostel, a number of restaurants, and during the summer there is also accommodation in the high school.

Tours from here can be arranged to the ghost towns of Avssakk'utak and Ikerasak. The first is about an hour's sailing away and contains many well preserved houses dating back to 1730, while Ikerasak is on the site of an ancient burial ground.

Igaliko

After a 90-minute boat trip, passengers have to walk several kilometres to get to this village where there are the ruins of the Norsemen's first cathedral and a bishop's tomb. If you are lucky they will lay on a tractor to take you back to the ship.

Inland Ice

A trip for good walkers who have to hike about 12km ($7^1/_2$ miles). The guided round trip takes between 6 and 8 hours.

Jakobshavn

(Greenland name Ilulissat) The name means the Ice Mountains, and the town is situated north of the famous Ice Fjord, from which some of the world's greatest icebergs are launched. It is a centre for the shrimp industry in the summer and halibut in the winter. Founded in 1741 by a trader Jakob Severen, it now has a population of 3,500 and is being groomed as a tourist destination. There are several helicopter flights each week. There are two hotels, both with restaurants and discos, and many well-preserved old buildings. There is the Knud Rasmussen Museum dedicated to the world famous explorer and writer.

Julianehab

(Greenland name Qaqortoq) Julianehab has a population of 3,000 and is the largest town in southern Greenland. Its main industries are fishing, sheep farming and canning. It was founded in 1775 by merchant Anders Olsen, and the town still has a number of well-preserved houses from this old town, and nearby there are remains of earlier Norse settlements, including the Hvalsey Church, probably the best preserved ruin from this period. In the town's market place is the Memorial Well, Greenland's only fountain. There is a hotel, hostel, restaurants and the Julianehab Museum, the largest local museum on the island, situated in an old smithy, showing how the Greenlanders used to live.

Narssaq

In the south-west corner of Greenland, this small town is

continued

PLACES TO VISIT
IN GREENLAND – Continued

surrounded by deep fjords. The island town and its surrounding mainland has a population of about 1,800, and fishing is the main industry, especially cod and shrimps, which are frozen or tinned and sent all over the world. The rest of the economy comes from farming, furs and semi-precious stones. There was a settlement here as far back as AD986. Today there are hotels, restaurants and shops, specialising in Eskimo crafts, precious stones and silver.

It is about an hour's walk to the small Eskimo village of **Cape Dan**, one of the most isolated settlements on earth. It was discovered by the Europeans in 1844 and the community was still 'living in the Stone Age'. The houses are still small and made of wood, and the cemetery, which you pass on the way into the village, consists of piles of stones. The ground is too hard to dig, so the coffins are laid on the ground and then covered with rocks. There are still less than 500 people in the village, mostly dependent on fishing and seal hunting, but bone carvings and bead ornaments are now being produced to sell to the tourists. After taking off and before heading back for Reykjavík, the plane normally circles over the village so you can see just how cut off it is.

Narssarssuaq
In the southern part of Greenland

on the Tunungdliarfik Fjord, named after Eirík the Red. There are also the remains of an Eskimo settlement which is thought to date back to the seventeenth century. The town, with a population of about 1,750 is 69km (43 miles) from the main coastline. During the last war a US airbase, Blue West One, was established there and it is now a weather and radio station. The town has two hotels, restaurants and just outside, a geophysical observatory and satellite station.

Qagssiarssuk
A sheepbreeding village about half an hour's sailing away, from Narssarssuaq and the site of Eirík the Red's farm. Ruins of the farm can still be seen as well as traces of the first Christian church in Greenland built by his wife, Tjodhild, in about 100. It was discovered during excavations which started in 1961.

Quoroq Fjord
At the end of this is an active glacier which throughout the summer feeds icebergs into the water.

Ulkebugten
Only an hour away from Holsteinsborg is a waterfall, the Ulkebugten, where in June you can find the yellow snow anemone, one of only two places on the island — the other being Evighedisfjord.

profitable. There is also lead and zinc at the Marmorilik mine, but this too is no longer profitable to extract. A massive 2 billion tons of iron ore has been located north of Godthab, and there are deposits of molybdenum, copper and scheelite on the east coast. None of these has yet been exploited, but uranium deposits near Narssaq may be tapped.

Greenland has most of what Iceland has to offer but it is bigger! It has the world's largest glacier, massive icebergs, a wealth of wildlife including reindeer, musk ox, polar bear, fox and polar hare and many rare birds, such as the snowy owl and sea eagle.

Flights from Reykjavík normally land at either Narssarssuaq, in the far south, or on the island of Kulusuk, in the entrance of Angmagssalik Fjord. There are a number of operators who offer flights to Greenland. Once you have arrived, it is possible to fly on with Greenlandair, who operate the world's largest fleet of helicopters. Reservations are essential on almost all of these internal flights.

Valid passports are required and special permits are needed if you want to travel near any of the military zones, around Søndre Strømfjord, with its US airforce base, or Thule. Permits can be obtained from Danish embassies.

There are hotels in all the main settlements, although standards vary and can be spartan. In smaller communities, there are often dormitories, rooms with four or more beds to a room. Standard cuisine varies from high in the better hotels to interesting. Local lamb, salmon and shrimps are all recommended, and you may like to try whale or seal meat.

Tipping is not obligatory but it is customary to add 10 per cent to taxi and restaurant bills. All alcohol is subject to a rationing system, and visitors can get their quota on presentation of their passport.

Souvenirs include sealskin goods, walrus ivory carvings and semi-precious stones and you can buy furs, but keep the receipt for Customs.

USEFUL INFORMATION

ACCOMMODATION

There is accommodation to suit all pockets in Iceland from luxury hotels to sleeping bag accommodation. Below is a list of guest houses, hotels and youth hostels of all kinds. A more comprehensive list can be obtained from tourist information offices.

Greater Reykjavík
City Hotel, Ránargata 4a
Holiday Inn, Sigtún 38
Hotel Borg, Pósthússtraeti 11
Hotel Esja, Sudurlandsbraut 2
Hotel Gardur, at Hringbraut
Hotel Geysir, Skipholt 27
Hotel Holt, Bergstadastræti 37
Hotel Lind, Raudarárstígur 18
Hotel Loftleidir, Reykjavík
  Airport

Hotel Ódinsvé, at Ódinstorg
Hotel Saga, Hagatorg
Salvation Army Guesthouse,
  Kirkjustræti 2
Guesthouse Mattheu,
  Bugdulækur 13
Guesthouse Snorra,
  Snorrabraut 61
Guesthouse Berg, Bæjarhraun
  4, Hafnarfjördur
Guesthouse Brautarholt 22
Guesthouse Flókagata 1
Guesthouse Flókagata 5
Guesthouse Mjóshlid 2
Guesthouse Svanurinn,
  Lokastigur 24a

The East
Hotel Tangi, Vopnafjördur
Hotel Egilsstadir, Egilsstadir
Hotel Valaskjálf, Egilsstadir
Hotel Snæfell, Seydisfjördur
Hotel Askja, Eskifjördur

Hotel Búdareyri, Reydarfjördur
Hotel K.H.B., Reydarfjördur
Hotel Bláfell, Breiddalsvík
Hotel Djúpivogur, Djúpivogur
Hotel Höfn, Hornafjördur
Hotel Edda, Hallormsstadur
Hotel Edda, Eidar
Hotel Edda, Nesjaskóla v/Höfn
Husmædraskólinn,
  Hallormsstadur
Brúarásskóli, Jökuldalur

The South
Hotel Valhöll, Thingvellir
Hotel Ljósbrá, Hveragerdi
Hotel Örk, Hveragerdi
Hotel Sellfoss, Selfossi
Hotel Thóristún, Selfoss
Hotel Edda, Laugarvatn
Hotel New Edda, Laugarvatn
Guesthouse Skálholt, Skálholt
Hotel/Motel Flúdir, Flúdir
Guesthouse Mosfell, Hella
Hotel Hvolsvöllur, Hvolsvöllur
Hotel Edda, Skógar
Guesthouse KS, Vík í Myrdalur
Hotel Edda, Kirkjubæjark-
  laustur
Hotel Gestgjafinn, Westman
  Islands
Guesthouse Skútinn, Westman
  Islands
Hotel Thórshamar, Westman
  Islands
Hotel Kristína, Njardvík
Hotel Keflavík, Keflavík
Flug Airport, Keflavík
Bláa Lónid, Svartsengi
Hotel Ósk, Akranes

The West
Hotel Akranes, Akranes
Hotel Borgarnes, Borgarnes
Hotel Bifröst, Hredavatn,
  Borgarfj
Hotel Edda, Reykholt
Hotel Búdir, Búdir, Snæfellsnes
Guesthouse Nes, Ólafsvík
Hotel Stykkishólmur,
  Stykkishólmur
Hotel Edda, Laugar,
  Sælingsdalur
Hotel Bjarkarlundur,
  Króksfjördur
Hotel Edda, Flókalundur,
  Vatnsfjördur
Hotel Ísafjördur, Ísafjördur
Hotel Ísafjördur, summer hotel
Guesthouse, Hólmavík
Hotel Búdardalur, Búdardalur

The North
Hotel Edda, Reykir,
  Hrútafjördur
Hotel Edda, Laugarbakki,
  Midfjördur
Vertshúsid, Hvammstangi
Hotel Blönduós, Blönduósi
Hotel Edda, Húnavellir,
  Svinadalur
Hotel Varmahlíd, Skagafjördur
Hotel Mælifell, Saudárkrókur
Hotel Torg, Saudárkrókur
Hotel Höfn, Siglufjördur
Hotel Ólafsfjördur, Ólafsfjördur
Guesthouse Víkurröst, Dalvík
Hotel Akureyri, Akureyri
Hotel Kea, Akureyri
Hotel Stefanía, Akureyri

Hotel Vardborg, Akureyri
Hotel Edda, Akureyri
Hotel Edda, Hrafnagil,
  Eyjafjördur
Hotel Edda, Stóru-Tjarnir,
  Ljósavatn
Hotel Laugar, S-Thingey-
  jarsysla
Hotel Húsavík, Húsavík
Hotel Reykjahlíd, Myvatn
Hotel Reynihlíd, Myvatn
Hotel Nordurljós, Raufarhöfn

Youth Hostels
The head office of the Iceland
YHA is at: Laufásvegur 41,101
Reykjavík, ☎ (91) 24950

Greenland's first hostel is at
Narssassuaq; central for
domestic travel, offering many
possibilities for hiking and
excursions to places of natural
and historical interest. The
hostel has excellent facilities
with a shop and tourist
information.

Akureyri
Stórholt 1,600 Akureyri

Lónsá Glæsibæjarhr, 601
Akureyri

Berunes
Beruneshr, S-Múl., 765
Djúpivogur

Breidavík
Raudasandshr.,
V-Bard, 451 Patreksfjördur

Fljótsdalur
Fljótshlíd, 861 Hvolsvöllur

Húsey
Hróarstunga, 701 Egilsstadir

Hveragerdi
Ból, Hveramörk 14, 810 Hveragerdi

Höfn
Nyibær, Hafnarbraut 8,780
Höfn

Leirubakki
Landssveit, Rang, 851 Hella

Reykholt
Biskupstungum, 801 Selfoss

Reykir
Sæberg, Hrútafjördur, 500 Brú

Reykjavík
Laufásvegur 41, 121 Reykjavík

Reykjavík
Sundlaugavegur 34, 105
Reykjavík

Reynisbrekka
Myrdalur, 870 Vík

Seydisfjördur
Hafaldan, 710 Seydisfjördur

Stafafell
Lón, 781 Höfn

Varmaland
Stafholtstunguhr., 311
Borgarnes

Vestmannaeyjar
Faxastígur 38, 900 Vestmannaeyjar

CHURCHES AND OTHER BUILDINGS OF INTEREST

Akureyri Church
Noted for its stained glass windows.

Bólstadur
Álftafjördur
Remains of tenth-century farm excavated in the 1920s.

Danish Merchant's House
Eyrarbakki
One of the oldest buildings in Iceland dating from 1765.

Glaumbaer
Collection of ancient and well-preserved farmhouses containing farmers' implements, clothing etc.

Gröf
Old farmhouse excavated from pumice which covered it in 1362.

Hallgrímskirkja
Njardargáta
Twentieth century
with lift to the steeple, giving magnificent view over the city.

Hof
Turf-roofed traditional church.

Hólar in Hjaltadalur
Oldest stone church in Iceland.

Langeyri
Old whaling station.

Lutheran Cathedral
Austurvöllur
Eighteenth century, much altered and renovated.

Nordic House
Njardargata
Reykjavík
☎ 91 17030
Built by Alvar Aalto, operated jointly by Nordic countries as a centre for Nordic culture.

Parliament House
(Althing)
Kirkjustræti
Reykjavík
Seat of the oldest legislative body in the world.

Skriduklaustur
Experimental farm on site of fifteenth-century monastery. Part of the buildings forms a folk museum.

DRIVING INFORMATION

1. Bringing Your Own Car
When bringing a car into the country one must produce the driver's passport and driving licence, the car's registration certificate (log book) and a green card. The car is examined and a temporary importa-

tion permit issued. Maximum dimensions are: Width = 2.5m, length = 13m. Vehicles which take fifteen or more passengers may not have trailers. Coach crew and passengers must leave the country with their vehicle.

Fuel may only be imported in the vehicle's fuel tanks (maximum 200 litres). Fishing equipment which has been used abroad will be sterilized at customs unless a valid sterilization certificate is produced. The import of weapons and drugs is not permitted.

Travellers aged 20 or over may import 1 litre of spirits and 1 litre of wine, or in place of either one of these a limited amount of alcoholic beer.

Most of the road surfaces are unmade and drivers should watch out for loose gravel at the road side. Gas containers should neither be stored under nor outside the vehicle. Mud flaps are compulsory, to minimise the chances of stones being thrown up in the path of oncoming vehicles. In dry weather dust from the roads can impair visibility and in some parts of the country sandstorms can hold up traffic for hours. There are free facilities for washing your car at filling stations.

2. Driving in Iceland

Most country roads are unmade and not suitable for fast driving. Speed limits are 50km/h (31mph) in built-up areas and 80/90km/h (50-56mph) on highways. Drive carefully and show consideration for other road users. Use headlights day and night — dust often impairs visibility. Decelerate and keep well to your side of the road when meeting oncoming traffic. Blind spots at the top of hills are common and not always marked. They are, however, usually marked with a 'danger ahead' sign (an exclamation mark within a triangle) and the word BLINDHÆD below.

Bridges usually only allow one lane of traffic. Many unbridged rivers appear quite safe at first sight but can prove extremely difficult once the crossing has been embarked on. Check carefully before fording the river, especially if there are no accompanying vehicles.

Get the latest information on mountain roads and tracks. They can be impassable long into the summer. Pay close attention to all road signs, especially on routes new to you. The use of seat belts in front seats is compulsory in Iceland, and the use of seat

belts in rear seats is encour-
aged.

Drinking and driving is
forbidden by law in Iceland.

3. The Interior

Once away from the main
roads the traveller will find
himself in uninhabited country,
mostly highland, where more
primitive conditions prevail,
with nature delicately balanced
and hardly any tourist services.
There are no shops and no
filling stations.

There are some travellers'
lodges in the interior but
members of the touring clubs
which own them take prefer-
ence for accommodation, so
one should book in advance at
the touring club office. Bring an
accurate map with you and
plan your route in advance.
Make enquiries about the situ-
ations you are likely to encounter and write an itinerary.
Remember that roads in the
interior are slower than the
highways so don't reckon a
day's journey on the basis of
kilometres.

In early summer when the
frozen earth is thawing, many
unmade roads can become
waterlogged and one can
expect some highways to be
closed for a time or for axle
weight restrictions to be

imposed (down to max. 5 tons
axle weight). Roads in the
interior are only passable by 4-
wheel drive vehicles and are
closed to all traffic until the first
week in July. Some roads in
the interior are not opened until
the middle of July, e.g. Land-
mannalaugar-Eldgjá,
Gæsavatnaleid, Kverkfjöll,
Snæfell and Fjallabaksleid
sydri. There are many unbridged rivers to be crossed in
the interior and they should be
treated with extreme caution.

Find out when the roads in
the interior are open (radio
broadcasts in English) and take
account of this when planning
your route. It is an offence not
to keep to the road when
driving (a measure taken when
it was realized how quickly
erosion took hold and spread
where car tracks on soft ground
and moss had left deep scars).
The police monitor traffic,
sometimes from the air, and
impose fines.

4. Driving in the Interior

It is essential to plan your
route, collect information about
it and find out how the roads
are before commencing your
journey. Enquire about weather
and road conditions on the
route you plan to travel. Take
warm clothes and rainwear and

all necessary equipment and spares for the car. When planning your route, take into account the fact that the roads in the interior are slower than the highways.

Check unbridged rivers by wading across them before attempting to drive over. Don't travel alone in the interior in winter, nor in the summer if the weather outlook is poor. If your vehicle gets stuck or breaks down, wait for help in the vehicle (it provides shelter). If the engine starts then don't waste fuel. Preserve heat and electricity. Put on warm clothing before you feel cold. Ration food and water.

Don't leave your vehicle unless you have given the matter considerable thought and never on your own. If the decision is taken to leave the vehicle, a note should always be left stating number of passengers, their names and ages, the time of departure from the vehicle and the intended destination.

Be on the lookout for search parties and remember that you will be more visible if you are wearing bright-coloured clothing.

5. Unbridged Rivers

When planning a trip in the interior it is necessary to find out if there are any unbridged rivers on the route and where the fords are. Accurate maps are available in the bookshops and at certain places in the interior there are wardens who know the condition of the rivers at any given time. Rivers often change course and an apparently harmless river can become a raging torrent almost without warning. Never take risks. If there is a lot of water in the river, wait until it subsides. Never attempt to cross a river unless another vehicle is waiting to assist if you get into difficulties.

Wade across the ford before attempting to drive over, and check the condition of the river bed. Look out for quicksand. The person who wades across the ford should wear a life jacket and be attached to a life line. The cold water in Icelandic rivers can cause cramp in those who fall in and even death. It is often difficult to see the river bed of glacial rivers as the water can be muddy. Check the strength of the current and its course. The best point to ford the river is not necessarily the narrowest. The one who wades the river should carry a pole to test the river bed and for support in strong currents. Face upstream in deep water and don't let the current hit you behind the knees.

Never assume that wheel marks leading into a river indicate that the river can be forded at that point. Never try to cross a river in a small low-powered car with an ill-pro-tected ignition system. (The ignition system can be pro-tected for a short while by covering the leads and distribu-tor with loose wool or other material.) Make sure the air intake is not submerged and switch off the lights when driving into cold water. Re-member that brakes often do not work for a short while after driving in water.

6. Spares and Safety Equipment
When you travel into the interior it is as well to keep in mind the fact that there are no shops and no repair services there. It is essential to carry both spares for the car and some safety equipment in case of mishap.

Spares
Distributor cap, rotor arm, con-densor, fan belt, spare plugs (4-8), fuel pipe, jubilee clips (various sizes), insulated wire, spare bulbs, lubricating oil for a complete all-round oil change, sealing compound for radiator and fuel tank, waterproofing spray for ignition system, penetrating oil, brake fluid, extra fuel, cotton waste or rags.

Safety Equipment
Tow rope, spade, crow bar, general purpose tool set, common bolts, nuts and screws, twine, jack, wheel brace, wheel nuts, good torch, batteries and bulbs, a good map of the area you are travelling in, waders, emer-gency rations, distress flares, extinguisher for general use, emergency radio transmitter or two-way radio.

EMBASSIES IN REYKJAVÍK

United Kingdom
Laufásvegur 49
☎ (91) 15883, 15884

USA
Laufásvegur 21
☎ (91) 29100

EMERGENCY SERVICES IN REYKJAVÍK

Ambulance ☎ (91) 11100
Fire department
☎ (91) 11100
Hospital — casualty ward
☎ (91) 696600

Medical help

weekdays 8am-5pm
☎ (91) 696600
weekdays 5pm-8am and
weekends ☎ (91) 21230

Pharmacies: at least one is
open 24 hrs. Look for
'Apótek' in the telephone
directory.

Police ☎ (91) 11166

Rescue squads ☎ (91) 27111

FERRIES IN ICELAND

Reykjavík-Akranes
- The Ferry Akraborg -
Cruising the Faxaflói
Summer schedule: June-
August.

Stykkishólmur-Flatey-Brjánslækur
- The Ferry Baldur -
Cruising the Breidafjördur
Summer schedule: June-
August

Ísafjördur-Ísafjardardjúp-Hornvík
- The Ferry Fagranes -
Cruising the Ísafjardardjúp
Summer schedule: 27 June-31
August

Árskógssandur-Hrísey Island
- The Ferry Sævar -
Cruising the Eyjafjördur

Porlákshöfn-Vestmannaeyjar Islands
- The Ferry Herjólfur -
Summer schedule: June-Sep-
tember

ICELANDAIR OFFICES

England
172 Tottenham Court Road
London W1PP 9LG
☎ 01 388 5346

Scotland
Room C 104 Admin Block 'C'
Glasgow airport,
Paisley pa 32 st.
☎ (041) 8484488

USA
c/o American Airlines
Prudential Plaza,
Prudential Building
Michigan and Randolph Str.
Chicago III 6060
☎ 1-800-223-5500

610b Fifth Avenue,
Rockefeller Center,
New York NY 10111-0334
☎ (212) 967 8888
☎ (800) 223 5500

c/o United Airlines Capital
Hilton Hotel
16th and K. Str. NW Washing-
ton DC 20006
☎ 1-800-223-5500

ICELAND TRAVEL CLUB

The Iceland Travel Club (patron: Magnús Magnússon) is open to anyone interested in Iceland. Members receive a quarterly newsletter, details of club meetings, tours, special offers etc. There is an information service, book and map service and special discounts. To join write to: The Iceland Travel Club, 3 Deynecourt, Harrow Park, Harrow-on-the-Hill, Middlesex HA1 3JE, England.

INFORMATION OFFICES IN ICELAND

Akranes
INFO, Faxabraut
1, 300 Akranes
☎ (93) 13313

Akureyri
INFO, Hafnarstræti 82,
600 Akureyri
☎ (96) 27733

Höfn
INFO, at the camping site
780 Höfn
☎ (97) 81701

Húsavík
Ferdaskrifstofa Húsavíkur,
Travel Bureau

Stórigardur 7,
640 Húsavík
☎ (96) 42100

Ísafjördur
Ferdaskrifstofa Vestfjarda,
Travel Bureau
Hafnarstræti 4,
400 Ísafjördur
☎ (94) 3557

Kirkkjubæjarklaustur
INFO, by the church
880 Kirkjubæjarklaustur
☎ (98) 74621

Myvatn
Eldá Travel Service
Myvatn,
660 Reykjahlíd
☎ (96) 44220

Reykjavík
Tourist Information Centre
Ingólfsstræti 5
101 Reykjavík
☎ (91) 623045

Saudárkrókur
Hotel Áning
550 Saudárkrókur
☎ (95) 6717

Seydisfjördur
Austfar, by the harbour
710 Seydisfjördur
☎ (97) 21111

Stykkishólmur
INFO, Adalgata 2
340 Stykkishólmur
☎ (94) 3557

Vík
INFO, at the camping site
870 Vík
☎ (98) 71345

INTERNAL TRAVEL BY BUS AND BY PLANE

AKUREYRI
Bus daily
Planes daily (6-7 flights)
AKRANES
Buses daily
Boat daily (3-5 sailings)
BLÖNDUÓS
Buses daily
Planes Tue., Wedn., Thur., Fri., Sun
BORGARNES
Buses daily
Búdir (Snæfellsnes)
Buses daily
EGILSSTADIR
Buses from Akureyri, daily
Buses from Höfn daily
Planes from Reykjavík daily (2-3 flights)
FAGURHÓLSMYRI
Buses Tue, Thur, Sat, in June, daily in July and August
GULLFOSS and GEYSIR
Buses daily
Conducted tours during season
HREDAVATN (Borgarfjördur)
Buses daily
HÚSAVÍK
Buses from Akureyri daily July-Sept.

Planes daily
HVALFJÖRDUR
Buses daily
HVERAGERDI
Buses daily
HVOLSVÖLLUR
Buses daily
HÖFN (Hornafjördur)
Buses Tue., Thur., Sat. in June, daily July and August.
Planes daily ex. Sat.
ÍSAFJÖRDUR
Buses Tue., Thur. July and August
Planes daily (2-3 flights)
KEFLAVÍK
Buses daily
KIRKJUBÆJARKLAUSTUR
Buses Tue., Thur., Sat. in June, daily July and August
LAUGARVATN
Buses daily in June, July and August
LAKE MYVATN
Buses daily from Akureyri
Buses daily from Húsavík, June-August
PATREKSFJÖRDUR
Buses Mon., Thur.
Planes Mon., Wed., Thu., Fri.
REYKHOLT (Borgarfjördur)
Buses daily
SAUDÁRKRÓKUR
Planes daily except Sat., Sunday
SELFOSS
Buses daily
SEYDISFJÖRDUR
Buses from Akureyri Wed.
Buses from Höfn Wed.

Buses from Egilsstadir daily
exc. Sat., Sun.
SIGLUFJÖRDUR
Buses from Varmahlíd, Tues.,
Wed., Fri.
Planes from Reykjavík daily
SKAFTAFELL
Buses Tue., Thur., Sat. in
June, daily July and August
STYKKISHÓLMUR
Buses daily
Planes daily exc. Sat.
THINGVELLIR
Buses daily
THORLÁKSHÖFN
Buses daily
VARMAHLÍD
Buses daily
VÍK (MYRDALUR)
Buses Tue., Thur., Sat. in
June, daily July and August
VESTMANNAEYJAR (West-
man Islands)
Planes daily (4 flights)
Boat daily from Thorlákshöfn
VOPNAFJÖRDUR
Buses from Húsavík Mon,
Wed.
Planes from Akureyri daily exc.
Sat., Sun.
Planes from Egilsstadir Mon.,
Wed., Fri.

THE LANGUAGE

A Guide to Icelandic Pronunciation

Vowels
a (a) as in English, father
á (au) as in English, now
e (e) when short (ie before two
consonants) as in English, get.
When long as in English, air.
é (jé) represents the sound of
English, yes, occasionally also
written je.
i (I) as in English, bid.
í (i) as in English, green
ö (o) as in English (not American) not
ó (ou) as in English, slow
u (Y) is not found in English,
but represents a sound like ü in
Küste.
ú (u) as in English, school
y (and y) are pronounced like i
and í respectively
æ (ai) as in English, high
au (öy) represents a sound not
found in English (ie it is not the
sound represented by au in
other languages), but closely
approximated by the French
feuille. It is composed of
Icelandic ö and í.
ei and ey (ei) similar to English,
hate, or Dutch ij in fijn.

Consonants
Icelandic has two letters of its
own which resemble 'þ' and 'd'
but must not be confused with
them. The crossed 'ð' letter is
pronounced like a hard 'th' as
in 'them', while the hooked 'þ'
is pronounced like a soft 'th' as
in 'thing'. They have been
printed as 'th' in the following
text.

j (j) like English y in yes.
v (v) is pronounced as in English
r (r) is trilled, as in Scotch, Spanish, etc.
ll is pronounced (dl) eg Hella (hedla), fjall (fjadl).
f before l or n is pronounced like b, eg Keflavík (kehblavik), Höfn (höbn).
rn is pronounced dn, eg barn, (badn).
rl is pronounced like Icelandic ll (dl), eg karl (man) (kadl).
p, t, and k when doubled or when followed by l or n are preceded by a breath of air known as 'pre-aspiration': eg epli (apple) is pronounced (ehpll), hætta (to stop) (haihta), takk (thank you) (tahk). Otherwise, most Icelandic consonants are pronounced like their English or German counterparts.

Useful Words and Phrases

N.B. The 'd' in nearly all these words transcribes 'ð', pronounced 'th' as in 'them'.

English — Icelandic
I — *ég*
she — *hún*
you — *thid*
you — *thú*
it — *thad*
they — *their/thær/thau*
he — *hann*
we — *vid*
What is your name? — *Hvad heitir pú?*
My name is ... — *Ég heiti ...*
Where are you from? — *Hvadan ert pú?*
I am from England — *Ég er frá Englandi*
Where do you live here? — *Hvar byrd thú hér?*
I live at Hotel Saga — *Ég by á Hótel Sögu*
Do you speak English? — *Talar thú ensku?*
Who is this? — *Hver er thetta?*
This is my — *thetta er*
brother — *bródir minn*
sister — *systir mín*
mother — *módir mín*
father — *fadir minn*
wife — *konan mín*
husband — *madurinn minn*
daughter — *dóttir mín*
son — *sonur minn*
friend — *vinur minn*
Can you tell me the way to Hotel Saga? — *Getur pú sagt mér hvar Hótel Saga er?*
How far is it? — *Hvad er langt thangad?*
Where does this bus go? — *Hvert fer thessi vagn?*
How much does it cost? — *Hvad kostar thad?*
Can you help me please? — *Getur thú hjálpad mér?*
Waiter! — *thjónn!*
What can I do for you? — *Hvad get ég gert fyrir thig*

I'd like some — *Ég ætla ad fá*
tea —*te*
coffee — *kaffi*
milk — *mjólk*
soda — *gosdrykk*
whisky — *whisky*
beef — *nautakjöt*
fish — *fisk*
lamb — *lambakjöt*
veal — *kálfakjöt*
pork — *svínakjöt*
a sandwich — *samloku*
an egg — *egg*

Thank you — *Takk fyrir*
Can I help you? — *Get ég adstodad?*
Yes, thank you — *Já, takk*
I'll have a kilo of apples — *Ég ætla ad fá kíló af eplum*
half a kilo of eggs — *Ég ætla ad fá hálft kíló af eggjum*
500 grams of oranges — *Ég ætla ad fá 500 grömm af appelsínum*
I'd like to look at some sweaters — *Get ég fengid ad lita á theysur?*
What colour? — *Hvada lit?*
a)blue b)green c)red)
d)yellow e)black f)white
g)grey h)brown i)violet
j)pink— *a)bláan b)grænan c)raudand)gulan e)svartan f)hvítang)gráan h)brúnann i)fjólu-bláan j)bleikan*
Which size? — *Hvada stærd?*
How much for a postcard/letter to England? — *Hvad kostar undir póstkort/bréf til Englands?*

20/30/40/50/60/70/80/90kr. — *tuttugu/thrjátíu/fjörutíu/fimmtíu/sextíu/sjötíul/áttatíu/nítíu kr.*
Where can I phone? — *Hvar get ég hringt?*
The number is 1-2-3-4-5-6-7-8-9-10-11-12 — *Númerid er einn-tveir-thrír-fjórir-fimm-sex-sjö-átta-níu-tíu-ellefu-tólf*

Your passport please — *Vegabréfid takk*
Fill in this form please — *Vildir thú fylla út eydubladid takk?*
Sign here please — *Skrifid undir hér*
Where is the next hotel/youth hostel/camping place? — *Hvar er næsta hótel/far fuglaheimili/tjaldstædi?*
Is there a hotel/youth hostel/camping place near here? — *Er hótel/farfuglaheimili/tjaldstædi hér nærri?*
Do you have two single rooms? — *Áttu tvö einstaklings herbergi?*
a double room? — *Áttu tveggja manna herbergi?*
For how many persons? — *Fyrir hve marga?*
How long will you stay? — *Hve lengi ætlid thid ad vera?*
Where is the toilet please? — *Hvar er badherbergid?*
dining room? — *matsalurinn?*

What is the matter? — *Hvad er ad?*

Where do you feel pain? —
Hvar finnur thú til?
In my arm — *Í handleggnum*
leg — *fætinum*
stomach — *maganum*
neck — *hálsinum*
head — *höfdinu*
back — *bakinu*
heart — *hjartanu*
I've got a toothache — *Ég er
med tannpínu*
headache — *höfudverk*
stomach ache — *magaverk*

MUSEUMS AND GALLERIES IN REYKJAVÍK

Árbær Open-air Museum
Árbær
☎ (91) 84412
Old buildings and artifacts
depicting life in Reykjavík
through the centuries.
Open: 10am-6pm daily except
Mondays. September, Satur-
day-Sunday 10am-6pm. From
October by arrangement only.

Árni Magnússon Institute
Sudurgata on the University
campus.
☎ (91) 25540
A research institute exhibiting
ancient Icelandic manuscripts.
Open: Tuesday, Thursday,
Saturday 2-4pm.
Group arrangements at other
times.

Ásgrímur Jónsson Museum
Bergstadastræti 74
☎ (91) 13644
Home and studio of the late
painter. Permanent display of
selected works.
Open: June-August 1.30-4pm
daily except Mondays. No
entrance fee.

Ásmundur Sveinsson House
(Gallery)
Freyjugata 41
☎ (91) 32155
Formerly home and studio of
late sculptor Ásmundur Sveinsson, presently owned by the
Association of Icelandic
Architects and used for various
exhibitions. Hours: decided by
each artist, please call to
check.

Ásmundur Sveinsson Museum
Sigtún
☎ (91) 32155
Collection of original sculptures
by Ásmundur Sveinsson,
indoors and out.
Open: 10am-4pm daily.

Einar Jónsson Museum
Njardargata
☎ (91) 13797
A large indoors/outdoors
collection of sculptures by
Einar Jónsson.
Open: Saturday-Sunday 1.30-
4pm.

FÍM Gallery
Gardarstræti 6
Open: 2-7pm during exhibitions.

Galleri Borg
Pósthússtræti 9
(at Austurvöllur) and
Austurstræti 10
☎ (91) 24211
Frequent exhibitions.
Open: Monday-Friday 10am-6pm, Saturday 10am-12noon.

Galleri Borg Grafík
Austurstræti 10
☎ (91) 24211
(entrance through the Penninn shop)
An annex from the Borg gallery at Pósthússtræti 9, by Austurvöllur, dedicated to the graphic arts. Selling works by almost all Icelandic artists in this field.
Open: normal shopping hours.

Galleri Gangskör
Amtmannsstígur 1
☎ (91) 13622
Entrance at Restaurant Torfan
Miscellaneous.
Open: Tuesday-Friday 12noon-6pm.

Galleri Grjót
Skólavördustígur 4a
☎ (91) 23707
Miscellaneous.

Open: Monday-Friday 12noon-6pm, Saturday 10am-4pm.

Galleri Gudmundur frá Middal
Skólavördustigur 43
☎ (91) 10980
Exhibiting and selling paintings and other objects of art by Icelandic artists.
Open: Monday-Friday 2-6pm, Saturday 10am-4pm.

Galleri Jens
(Jens Gudjónsson - silversmith/jeweller)
Stigahlíd 45-47
☎ (91) 36778
Adjacent to owner's workshop. Gold and silver objects, plus miscellaneous art work by various artists: collage, sculptures, jewellery, mixed technique.
Open: Monday-Friday 9am-5pm.

Galleri List (Gallery Art)
Skipholt 50b
☎ (91) 84020
Close to Holiday Inn, Hotel Esja, Hotel Lind and Hotel Geysir.
Paintings, water colours, graphics, ceramics, glass and textiles by Icelandic artists. Frequent exhibitions.
Open: Monday-Friday 10am-6pm, Saturday 10am-12noon.

Galserí Svart á Hvitu
(Black on White)
Laufásvegur 17
☎ (91) 22611
Frequent exhibitions of various art forms.
Open: 2-6pm daily except Mondays.

Hafnar Gallerí
Hafnarstræti 4
☎ (91) 13133
A small new gallery for younger artists, operated by the Snæbjörn Jónsson Bookshop.
Open: normal business hours.

Hafnarborg
Strandgata 34
Hafnarfjördur
☎ (91) 50080
A brand new arts centre.

Hladvarpinn
Vesturgata 3
☎ (91) 19055
The Women's Centre, theatre and exhibition hall.

Hulduhólar
Mosfellssveit
by the highway
(about 10min drive)
☎ (91) 666194
Ceramics. Owner/workshop.
Open: daily but irregular, advisable to call for appointment.

Icelandic Art Gallery
Vesturgata 17
☎ (91) 10661

Kjarvalsstadir
Miklatún
☎ (91) 26131
The Municipal Art Gallery built in honour of Jóhannes Sveinsson Kjarval, Iceland's legendary painter. One of the building's two large exhibition halls is almost solely dedicated to Kjarval's art.
Open: 2-10pm daily, cafeteria 2-7pm.

Kogga
Vesturgata 5
☎ (91) 26036
Ceramics. Owner/workshop.
Open: Monday-Friday 9am-6pm, Saturday irregular.

Labour Unions' Art Gallery
Grensásvegur 16, top floor
☎ (91) 681770
Large collection of art, largely paintings.
Open: Monday-Friday 4-8pm, weekends 2-10pm.

Maritime Museum
Vesturgata 8
Hafnarfjörder
☎ (91) 52502
Open: until end September, 2-6pm daily except Mondays. From October, Saturday/Sunday 2-6pm.

National Gallery of Iceland
Fríkirkjuvegur 7
☎ (91) 621000
A comprehensive collection of
Icelandic art.
Open: museum, cafeteria and
library 11.30am-4.30pm daily,
except Mondays.

National Museum of Iceland
Sudurgata
☎ (91) 22220
Open: until mid-September:
11am-4pm daily except
Monday. From mid-September
Sunday, Tuesday, Thursday,
Saturday 11am-4pm.

Natural History Museum
at Hlemmtorg
☎ (91) 29822
Open: Sunday, Tuesday,
Thursday and Saturday 1.30-
4pm.

Nature Study Centre
Digranesvegur 12
Kópavogur
☎ (91) 40630
Open: Saturday 2.30-4.30pm
and for groups on other days/
hours on request.

Nordic House
Hringbraut
close to the university campus
☎ (91) 17030
Cultural forum for the Nordic
nations. Includes library,
cafeteria, exhibition rooms and
lecture/recital hall.
Open: cafeteria Monday-Friday
9am-5pm, Saturday 9am-7pm
and Sunday 12noon-7pm;
library Monday-Saturday 1-
7pm, Sunday 2-5pm; exhibition
halls 2-7pm daily during
exhibitions.

Numismatic Museum
(coin and bank note collection)
Einholt 4
☎ (91) 699600
Joint venture by the National
Museum of Iceland and the
Central Bank of Iceland.
Open: regular hours: 2-4pm
Sundays. Open on request
during the week.

Nyhöfn Gallery
Hafnarstræti 18
Across from the Rammagerdin
store
☎ (91) 12230
An art gallery in the centre of
Reykjavík exhibiting and selling
paintings, graphics and other
objects of art by contemporary
Icelandic artists.
Open: Monday-Friday 10am-
6pm and Saturday-Sunday
2-6pm during exhibitions.
Saturday and Sunday closed in
July and August.

Nylistasafnid
(The Living Art Gallery)
Vatnsstigur 3b
☎ (91) 14350

An avant-garde inclined organization.
Open: Monday-Friday 4-8pm, weekends 2-8pm.

Post and Telecommunication History Museum
Austurgata 11
Hafnarfjördur
A collection of artifacts depicting the development of postal and telephone services in Iceland through the centuries.
Open: Sunday and Tuesday 3-6pm. Open on request outside regular hours,
☎ (91) 54321.

Pyrít
Vesturgata 3
☎ (91) 20376
Gallery/workshop for goldsmith/jeweller, Anna María Sveinbjörnsdóttir.

University Gallery
On the University campus, right across from the Nordic House
Open: daily 1-5pm.

OTHER MUSEUMS

Akranes
Folk Museum

Borgarnes
Natural history/folk museum

Eskifjördur
Folk and nautical museum

Glaumbaer
Folk museum

Heimaey
Westman Islands
Folk museum
Natural history museum

Hellisandur
Nautical museum

Hnjótur
Folk museum

Höfn
Folk museum

Ísafjördur
Local folk museum

Keflavík
Folk museum

Kópavogur
Natural history museum

Laugár
Folk museum

Neskaupstadur
Natural history museum

Ólafsvík
Unique storage house built in 1841 now a local craft museum.
Maritime museum.

Reykir
Folk museum

Rjómabúid
Stokkseyri
An interesting folk museum

Saudárkrókur
Art museum

Selfoss
Folk museum
Art gallery

Skógar
Local museum

Thorlákshöfn
Folk museum

PLACES OF INTEREST IN AKUREYRI

Botanical Garden
A live plant collection where
you can find a specimen of
every flower and plant that
grows in Iceland. Open daily
during the summer 9am-10pm.

Davídshús
(The Davíd Stefánsson Memorial Museum)
6 Bjarkarstigur
The home of the poet Davíd
Stefánsson, where you can see
his furniture, his books and
some of his other personal
belongings. Open daily June-
September, 4-6pm.

The Folklore Museum
58 Adalstræti
Here you will find furniture,
ornaments and other items of
historical interest from Akureyri
and the surrounding district.
Souvenir shop.
Open: daily June-September
1-5pm.

Fridbjarnarhús
(I.O.G.T. Museum)
46 Adalstræti
Open: Sundays during July and
August 2-5pm. Objects and
pictures in every room of the
house, relating to the activities
of the Organisation of Good
Templars.

**The Museum of Natural
History**
81 Hafnarstræti
An excellent collection of
Icelandic birds and a scientifi-
cally classified plant collection.
Open June-September, daily
except Saturdays 11am-2pm.
(During the winter, Sundays
1-7pm.)

Nonnahus
(The Jón Sveinsson Memorial
Museum)
54b Adalstræti
The early home of Pater Jón
Sveinsson, whose books about
his youth and childhood in
Akureyri have been translated

into more than 40 languages.
Open: daily June-August,
2-4.30pm.

Sigurhædir

(The Matthias Jochumsson
Memorial Museum)
3 Eyrarlandsvegur
The home of the poet Matthias
Jochumsson, who translated
some of Shakespeare's works
into Icelandic.
Open: daily June-September,
2-4pm.

Town Library

17 Brekkugata
Open: during the summer,
Monday-Friday 1-7pm (during
the winter Saturdays also
10am-3pm).

PARKS AND BOTANICAL GARDENS

Akureyri Park

Opened in 1912, it has a
specimen of every flower and
plant which grows in Iceland.

Eden Garden Centre

Krísuvík
Glasshouses which enable
exotic fruit to be grown. Area
has shops and cafés making
an agreeable visit.

Jökulsárgljufur National Park

Reykjavík Botanical Garden

Laugardalur
Reykjavík
Open: daily in summer 9am-
10pm.
Botanical garden near outdoor
sports stadium.

Skaftafell National Park

Skaftafell
National Park created in 1967.
Rich in unique flora and fauna.
Campsite. Warden on duty in
summer months.

Thingvellir National Park

TOUR OPERATORS

For details of holidays to
Iceland, any of the following
tour operators will be pleased
to assist you.

Arctic Experience Ltd
29 Nork Way, Banstead
Surrey SM7 1PB
☎ 07373 62321

Explore Worldwide
7 High Street, Aldershot
Hampshire GU11 1BH
☎ 0252 319448

Finlandia Travel
130 Jermyn Street
London SW1Y 4UJ
☎ 01-839 4741

Donald Mackenzie (Travel) Ltd
144 St Vincent Street
Glasgow G2 5LH
☎ 041-248 7781

Mason International Travel
79 Hope Street
Glasgow G2 6AJ
☎ 041-248 3166
Mays Holidays
22 Royal Crescent
Glasgow G3 7SZ
☎ 041-331 1200

Dick Phillips
Whitehall House, Nenthead,
Alston
Cumbria CA9 3PS
☎ 0498 81440

Regent Holidays
66 Regent Street, Shanklin
Isle of Wight PO37 7AE
☎ 098386 4212
Also at:
13 Small Street
Bristol BS1 1DE
☎ 0272 211711

Scanscape Holidays
197-199 City Road
London EC1V 1JN
☎ 01-251 2500

Scantours
8 Spring Gardens
Trafalgar Square
London SW1A 2BG
☎ 01-839 2927

Twickenham Travel
33 Notting Hill Gate
London W11 3JQ

☎ 01-568 5581
Also at:
5 Royal Exchange Square
Glasgow G1 3AN
☎ 041-204 0242

Twickers World
22 Church Street, Twickenham
Middlesex TW1 3NW
☎ 01-892 7606

Vardon Travel
50A Fenchurch Street
London EC3M 3JY
☎ 01-839 2927

Waymark Holidays
295 Lillie Road
London SW6 7LL
☎ 01-385 5015

YHA Travel
14 Southampton Street
London WC2E 7HY
☎ 01-836 8541

USEFUL ADDRESSES

Iceland Tourist Board
172 Tottenham Court Road
London W1P 9LG
☎ 01-388 5599

Iceland Tourist Board
360 West 31st Street
4th Floor
New York
NY 10001-2793
USA
☎ 010-212-1400 (reception)

INDEX